I0081735

The One Woman Show
A New Voice in the Desegregation Movement

Jessica J. Davis, J.D., D.Min., Ph.D.

Faith and Public Policy Institute
Princeton

Names: Davis, Jessica J. (Jessica June), 1968- | Davis, Jessica J.
    (Jessica June), 1968- Historical narrative on the role of Mrs.
    Esther Brown in the development of desegregation policy in
    public education.
Title: The one woman show : a new voice in the desegregation
    movement / Jessica J. Davis, J.D., D.Min., Ph.D.
Description: Princeton, New Jersey : Faith and Public Policy
    Institute, [2016] | "Adapted from A Historical Narrative on
    the Role of Mrs. Esther Brown in the Development of
    Desegregation Policy in Public Education (Davis, 2016)"--
    Title page verso. | Includes bibliographical references and
    index.
Identifiers: ISBN 978-0-692-80558-9 | ISBN 0-692-80558-3
Subjects: LCSH: Brown, Esther, 1917-1970--Political and social
    views. | School integration--United States--History--20th
    century. | Public schools--United States--History--20th
    century. | Civil rights--United States--History--20th century.
Classification: LCC LC214.2 .D38 2016 | DDC 370.19342--dc23

Adapted from
*A Historical Narrative on the Role of Mrs. Esther Brown in the
Development of Desegregation Policy in Public Education* (Davis, 2016)
Copyright © 2016 Jessica Davis.
All rights reserved. No part of this book may be reproduced or
utilized in any form or by any means, electronic or mechanical,
including photocopying, recording, or by any information storage
and retrieval system without permission in writing from the
publisher.
Faith and Public Policy Institute, Inc.
Princeton, New Jersey
www.FaithPolicyInstitute.org

DEDICATION

In Memory of Mrs. Esther Brown
September 19, 1917- May 24, 1970

TABLE OF CONTENTS

ACKNOWLEDGMENTS

SOUTHERN ILLINOIS UNIVERSITY
CARBONDALE FACULTY

Dr. Saran Donahoo
Dr. Joseph A. Brown
Dr. Kay J. Carr
Dr. Judith A. Green
Dr. Sosanya Jones

CHAPTER 1

INTRODUCTION

The landmark civil rights case, *Brown v. Board of Education* (1954), is one of the most significant decisions of the twentieth century as it leads to the development of the desegregation policy for public education in the United States from the 1950s to the present (Manz, 2004). On November 13, 2002, the U.S. Secretary of Education, Rod Paige, described *Brown* as one of the greatest decisions of the Supreme Court and states in commemoration of the 50th anniversary of *Brown v. Board of Education*: "Education is a civil right. To deny that right is to cancel all rights. An educated child is a child who can grow up to be a full participant in society, voting, finding meaningful work, getting involved in the community, and working to achieve his or her own dream" (Paige, 2002). The same sentiment about education described by Secretary Paige echoes in the annals of the late 1940s through the 1950s with the civil rights activism of Mrs. Esther E. Brown, a heroine in the desegregation of public education. She is not related to the plaintiffs of *Brown v. Board of Education* (1954). She is only related to the plaintiffs in that both were in pursuit of racial equality in public education in the 1950s.

Mrs. Esther Brown, a White Jewish woman, made a significant contribution to the desegregation of public education in the 1940s and 1950s. Her contribution to the end of segregation policy in public education was essential, as she took the initiative to fight for equality in education for all children, irrespective of their racial background. After Mrs. Brown saw the poor learning conditions in a segregated South Park, Kansas school for African American students that lacked basic facilities, teachers, and other fundamental resources for learning, the fight for change ultimately drove her. As a result, she mobilized a group of African American parents and residents, and challenged the segregation policy in public education in her school district. She also planned and organized the boycott of the segregated Walker School and laid down strategies to raise money and public awareness regarding the inhumane practice of segregation in public education, which she insisted violated human rights provisions of equality (Byrne, Williams, & Thurgood Marshall Scholarship Fund, 2005).

The most influential action that Mrs. Brown took was putting together a historic lawsuit against the South Park school district. Consequently, she experienced a range of threats, harassments, and family problems, including her husband leaving. However, she pressed on and fought segregation at the South Park School, among other public schools where African American students received their education. Eventually, she succeeded with regard to public education desegregation in South Park. She immediately followed her success in desegregating South Park with her leadership in *Brown v. Board of Education* (1954), which ended in victory and the implementation of desegregation policy in public schools across the nation. As such, it is evident that Mrs. Brown's role was essential in the development of desegregation policy from its initial stages to full recognition and practice within schools throughout the nation (Claire & Lydia, 2011).

The desegregation of public education in America in the 1950s depended on an active collaboration between the Black community and their allies across the nation (Tyack & Lowe, 1986). Mrs. Esther Brown became one of the "white allies" in her pursuit for equal protection under the law in public education, first in Topeka, Kansas and then across the nation (Meier, 1963).

This historical narrative gives Mrs. Brown her rightful place in the contemporary public narrative on the development of desegregation policy in public education. Mrs. Brown's story of activism is not just important for the purpose of providing a more accurate account of the historical record on leaders and pioneers during this period of history but her story also provides a contemporary model for social activism. She shows what one person can accomplish in the face of social injustice.

CHAPTER 2

MRS. ESTHER BROWN

Mrs. Esther E. Brown is one of the unsung heroines and pioneers of local civil rights activism that changed the national landscape of public education in the 1950s. The primary historical records actually reveal the depth of her leadership role ranging from being one of the founders of a local chapter of the NAACP in Kansas to becoming a regional fundraiser in order to pay the fees of the legal counsel in the campaign to change local public education policy in the 1950s in Kansas. However, Mrs. Brown is only mentioned briefly in five separate short published texts ranging from one page to twelve pages with pictures in the volumes of contemporary public narratives on the development of the desegregation policy in public education in the 1950s that historians and scholars have written over the last fifty years (Katz & Tucker, Winter 1995/1996; Kaufman, 1989; Kluger, 2004; Speer, 1968; The JBHE Foundation, 2001). According to the brief one page historical statement in *The Journal of Blacks in Higher Education* (2001), Mrs. Brown actually organized the first major U.S. challenge to racial segregation in public education. This historical narrative will give Mrs. Brown her rightful place as one of the leaders in the contemporary public narrative on the history of the development of desegregation policy in public education in the United States in the late 1940s and early 1950s.

In 1947, Mrs. Brown, a hazel-eyed, curly-headed brunette of thirty, was a suburban housewife and mother of two young daughters from Merriam, Kansas, an area southwest of Kansas City, who challenged racial segregation in public schools from the late 1940s through the 1950s. She was an American-born Jewish woman but the daughter of Russian-Jewish immigrants. She was born in Kansas City, Missouri on September 19, 1917 as Esther Swirk. Her mother died from cancer when she was 10 years old. Her father, Ben Swirk, raised Esther by himself after the death of her mother.

Ben Swirk, a watchmaker, was a member of several left-wing labor organizations including the International Workers Order and the Human Rights Club. Esther identified with her father's social activism and started participating in leftist activities during her high school years. She joined in a picket of garment workers in Chicago. She spent two summers at the leftist Commonwealth College in Mena, Arkansas. During these years, she also supported a group called the Spanish Loyalists. She attended both the University of Chicago and Northwestern University. Esther Brown's social consciousness started as a young girl in her working-class neighborhood of Kansas City, Missouri and continued throughout her life. In 1943, she married her childhood friend, Lieutenant Paul Brown, at the age of 26 years old. They moved to Merriam, Kansas after the war in the late 1940s where she launched her civil rights activism (Katz & Tucker, Winter 1995/1996; Kaufman, 1989; Kluger, 2004; Speer, 1968; The JBHE Foundation, 2001).

In 1947, Mrs. Brown's Black housekeeper, Mrs. Helen Swan, made Mrs. Brown aware of the segregation policies in their local school district while

Mrs. Brown was driving her home to the adjacent unincorporated township of South Park. Mrs. Swan informed Mrs. Brown that the school district approved a $90,000 bond to build a new school for the 222 White children in the district while leaving the 44 Black children in the same district in their 60 year old two-room schoolhouse, the Walker School named after Madame Walker, a Black businesswoman who made a fortune from developing hair products and cosmetics. Mrs. Brown's housekeeper also informed her of the inhumane conditions of the Walker School. She stated that the school was a rat infested dilapidated wooden two-room schoolhouse with no indoor plumbing. The students had to use an outhouse. She also told Mrs. Brown about the cafeteria in the tiny basement room of the schoolhouse flooding periodically. Mrs. Brown became outraged when she heard about the condition of the schoolhouse the school district used for the Black children in the district and the segregation policy being used to justify these conditions (Katz & Tucker, Winter 1995/1996; Kaufman, 1989; Kluger, 2004; Speer, 1968; The JBHE Foundation, 2001).

In response to the state of affairs of her school district, Mrs. Brown launched a campaign to challenge the school district's Jim Crow policies. She went door to door to organize the Black community in her school district. The leadership of the Black community expressed fear of retaliation by the school board. However, she aggressively lobbied the local school board to change their segregation policies. She organized a local chapter of the NAACP and then lobbied the New York NAACP headquarters to provide both financial and legal support. Her NAACP lobbying included pleading with Thurgood Marshall to send assistance to Kansas. Mrs. Brown also organized a successful home-school program in the Black community as a way to boycott the school district until they allowed Black children into the all-white school. Mrs. Brown traveled across the state to raise money for the home-school program (Katz & Tucker, Winter 1995/1996; Kaufman, 1989; Kluger, 2004; Speer, 1968; The JBHE Foundation, 2001).

Mrs. Brown was threatened repeatedly by members of the White community for her local activism including a cross burning on the lawn of her home. Mrs. Brown's local activism also led to a federal investigation by the Federal Bureau of Investigation (FBI) because of her local activism in the Black community of South Park. The FBI investigated Mrs. Brown and her husband as communist sympathizers which resulted in her husband losing his job and standing before a military tribunal fighting a dishonorable discharge from his position as a captain in the Air Force Reserves. Mrs. Brown also had a miscarriage during this tumultuous time of local activism (Katz & Tucker, Winter 1995/1996; Kaufman, 1989; Kluger, 2004; Speer, 1968; The JBHE Foundation, 2001).

However, Mrs. Brown's local activism led to a successful lawsuit, *Webb v. School District No. 90* (1949), in which the Court ordered the suburban school district of Merriam to integrate their all-white school. This court decision occurred five years before the Supreme Court's decision in *Brown v. Board of Education* (1954). Mrs. Brown did not stop with the success of *Webb v. School District No. 90 (1949).* She wanted to desegregate public schools across the state of Kansas. She started working with the NAACP in Topeka, Kansas after the success of the Merriam case. In Topeka, she helped to identify several Black families who could serve as potential plaintiffs in a case to challenge Topeka's racially desegregated school system. One of the families, Oliver Brown, a railroad welder and minister, became the plaintiff on behalf of her daughter, Linda Brown, for the landmark case, *Brown v. Board of Education* (1954). Mrs. Esther E. Brown lobbied the Legal Defense Fund to help with the litigation of this landmark case. In 1954, the decision of this landmark case outlawed racial segregation in all public schools across the nation. The secretary of the Topeka NAACP branch, Lucinda Todd, did not believe the landmark civil rights case would have occurred without Mrs. Brown's leadership. (Katz & Tucker, Winter 1995/1996; Kaufman, 1989; Kluger, 2004; Speer, 1968; The JBHE Foundation, 2001).

CHAPTER 3
ROOTS OF ACTIVISM

Mrs. Esther Brown, born Esther Swirk to Russian-Jewish immigrants on September 19, 1917, lived a working-class life in a Kansas City neighborhood in Missouri. Esther lost her mother to cancer at the age of ten, and her father, Ben Swirk, raised her from that point. Her father, a watchmaker, became very influential in her early activism. Socially conscious, Ben Swirk imparted his activism to his young daughter as he became a member of leftist labor organizations like the International Workers Order and the Human Rights Club. Although not a religious man, Mr. Swirk passed on strong Jewish ethical values to his daughter and Esther, influenced by this, took up activism herself. Even as a mere high school student, Esther joined a picket line of workers to protest injustice. In Chicago, at Marshall Fields, while working as a sales girl, she sympathized with garment workers by joining their picket line. She also enrolled for two summers at a labor-oriented institution, the Commonwealth College in Mena, Arkansas. The College, in its final years, was the venue for a strike staged by communist students who were fighting for the enrollment of a Black student, whom the administration refused to admit and Esther witnessed this early attempt at integration while she was attending college. She continued to espouse progressive stances on a number of political causes as a young adult (Katz & Tucker, 1995/1996; Kaufman, 1989; Kluger, 2004; Speer, 1968; The JBHE Foundation, 2001).

Bringing back these experiences and principles to her home city in Kansas, Missouri, Esther was dismissed from her new job at the Works Projects Administration, the largest New Deal agency employing millions for public works projects, based on her political beliefs. However, during this time, a childhood friend, Lieutenant Paul Brown, on leave from the army corps, redirected her passion for social activism to family life for a season when he married her. They moved to Kansas City, Kansas after the war with their two young daughters and settled in an unpretentious house in Merriam. It took more than a year living in Merriam before she would become involved in the legal case against segregation in South Park (Katz & Tucker, 1995/1996; Kaufman, 1989; Kluger, 2004; Speer, 1968; The JBHE Foundation, 2001).

CHAPTER 4

SOUTH PARK TOWNSHIP

Founded in the late nineteenth century, South Park Township was home to both Black and White residents. Less than a year after the local government established South Park in 1887, it became the jurisdiction of Johnson County School District No. 90, and the district constructed a one-room school for the education of both Black and White children. In 1900, South Park had 250 residents, including four "Negro" families who wanted a better life after suffering racial oppression in the south. In 1912, however, the school district segregated the once integrated community when they built a school exclusively for White children. Children of Black parents continued to stay in the older facility, which underwent building improvements in the 1920s. The school board did not have any record of any protests connected to this policy of segregation until 1947 when Esther Brown began challenging the desegregation policy of South Park (Katz & Tucker, 1995/1996; Kaufman, 1989; Kluger, 2004; Speer, 1968; The JBHE Foundation, 2001).

The school district housed the segregated Black school called the Walker School, in South Park, in a 60-year-old, run down building. It was named after Madame C.J. Walker, the first American female self-made millionaire who developed beauty and hair products for black women (Katz & Tucker, 1995). In Mrs. Esther Brown's personal conversations with her maid, Helen Swan, Mrs. Brown became aware of this segregated school's dilapidated condition. Mrs. Brown learned that the school board was planning to build a new school for the White children at the cost of $90,000 upon the approval of a bond with no provision whatsoever for similar improvements to the Black school (Brown, 1948c). The Black community was furious about this unjust use of taxes since they also paid the same taxes for the construction of the new school. Not long after, Mrs. Brown visited the school and saw with her own eyes the dilapidated, neglected building. The school consisted of two poorly heated rooms, a constantly flooded basement, and an outhouse.

In early October 1948, the school district authorities and two leaders of the Black community arranged a meeting. Helen Swan and Alfonso Webb, a Black contractor and a father of nine children, represented the Black community. The school district director Virgil Wisecup, board member Vernon Hoyt, and architect B.A. Larson represented the school district. Mrs. Swan and Mr. Webb explained that they only wanted improvements for the Walker School building, and not integration. The school board said that they also wanted to do the improvements but there was no money, and advised them to collect donations from their churches. As a measly token of their superficial desire to improve the school, months later, the board offered to put up a new mailbox and stop sign at the school (Brown, 1948c).

When Mrs. Brown saw that the school board did not take the Black community seriously, she met with Black leaders and put forth the idea of forming a local NAACP chapter in Merriam. Mrs. Brown argued that with the NAACP behind them, the school board would give their demands the attention they deserved. The suggestion was widely welcomed, and so in January 1948, Mr. Webb and Mrs. Brown met Rev. E.A. Freeman, president of the NAACP branch in Kansas City, who gave them his full support and the approval they needed to establish a new chapter in Merriam. The NAACP state president, A. Porter Davis, went to the first meeting with a promise to fully cooperate. Mr. Webb became the first chapter president. The chapter quickly grew to thirty members by February 1948 (Katz & Tucker, 1995/1996; Kaufman, 1989; Kluger, 2004; Speer, 1968; The JBHE Foundation, 2001).

To air their demands forcefully, the chapter hired the services of a lawyer, William Towers from Wyandotte County. Attorney Towers met with the school board and insisted on Mrs. Brown's demand of refurbishing the Walker School to the same degree as the South Park's new school building. The board quickly postponed the discussion to another meeting, which the board announced the following week with short notice. When Attorney Towers unexpectedly asked for additional legal fees to continue his representation, Mrs. Brown volunteered to represent the Black community along with her maid, Helen Swan, and her husband, William. At the meeting, they stressed that Black parents only wanted a better education for their children. Mrs. Brown argued that the board could not guarantee an equal education in two dilapidated classrooms for eight different grade levels managed by two teachers, one of whom was not even qualified to teach. The board responded through the principal for both schools, Mr. Edwin Campbell, by denying that unequal conditions existed between the two schools, and then making an insulting offer to install new lightbulbs, provide used desks from the old White school and promising to build a new school after the final payment of the bond in thirty years (Katz & Tucker, 1995/1996; Kaufman, 1989; Kluger, 2004; Speer, 1968; The JBHE Foundation, 2001).

All of these offers by the school board were unacceptable to Mrs. Brown and the Black parents, and they quickly communicated their disappointment to the school board. Mrs. Brown began receiving verbal threats from the White community due to her involvement in the school board complaint. A day after the unsuccessful board meeting, Mrs. Brown received a phone call from Mr. Larson, a school board member, telling her to stay away from this case. He then communicated an incident in which a White pharmacist speaking on behalf the Black community became a victim of a White embargo and how the community forced him to close shop and leave town (Katz & Tucker, Winter 1995/1996; Kaufman, 1989; Kluger, 2004; Speer, 1968; The JBHE Foundation, 2001).

A few weeks later, the school board chairman invited Mrs. Brown to a dinner at South Park School. Although Mrs. Brown's maid and husband tried to persuade her not to attend, she accepted the invitation to the dinner. However, when Mrs. Brown arrived she found, to her surprise, hundreds of people in the school's gymnasium. The bigoted board chairman opened with racist remarks and stated that as long as he was alive he would never allow Black students to enter South Park. Then the chair proceeded to elicit slurs and obscenities from the audience. Then suddenly, the gymnasium became quiet because they were expecting

Mrs. Brown to speak. Mrs. Brown gathered her strength and explained her side, but instead of showing their understanding, the audience became even more hostile towards her. A woman actually began hitting Mrs. Brown with an umbrella. Racist hoots, boos and shouts greeted her after her sincere speech. A Methodist minister tried to intervene, but when he attempted to calm the crowd, they gave him the same violent and rude treatment. Mrs. Brown publicly complained to the board about how they treated her so disrespectfully, especially since the chair of the board invited her, which he vehemently denied. (Katz & Tucker, 1995/1996; Kaufman, 1989; Kluger, 2004; Speer, 1968; The JBHE Foundation, 2001).

Mrs. Brown quickly realized that the school board staged the event to discourage her from leading the desegregation movement in South Park intended to equalize the educational opportunities between Black and White students. However, instead of intimidating her, Mrs. Brown left the gymnasium even more determined than before the hostile attack (Katz & Tucker, 1995, p. 239). After the incident, which was a turning point in her activist thinking, she became more convinced that only seeking equality would never work as long as the South Park community maintained segregated institutions like the public schools. Mrs. Brown concluded that the best way to combat racial inequality in South Park was to fight the segregation policy in public education by advocating for the integration of the Black Walker School and the White South Park School (Katz & Tucker, 1995/1996; Kaufman, 1989; Kluger, 2004; Speer, 1968; The JBHE Foundation, 2001).

After the staged board meeting, Mrs. Brown received daily phone calls at her home threatening her and her family. Then they followed the calls with threats of a house burning and a warning that the Ku Klux Klan may burn a cross on her lawn; the latter happened a few days later. Refusing to allow these threats to intimidate her, Mrs. Brown organized the Black community in Merriam and partnered with national NAACP leaders to take more decisive action. Instead of asking for better educational facilities and teachers at the Walker school, they demanded that Black children be admitted to the new South Park Common Grade School (Katz & Tucker, Winter

1995/1996; Kaufman, 1989; Kluger, 2004; Speer, 1968; The JBHE Foundation, 2001).

At the annual meeting of the school board on April 9, 1948, Esther Brown, Helen Swan and Alfonso Webb formally presented their demand for school desegregation, which the board met with outright rejection. When Mrs. Brown, Mrs. Swan, and Mr. Webb suggested that the board submit their request for desegregation to the district's voters, the board refused immediately. The school board and the White community met their demands for desegregation with vicious resistance. To fortify their position and establish their right to segregation, the school board concocted a zoning plan to maintain school segregation (Katz & Tucker, 1995/1996; Kaufman, 1989; Kluger, 2004; Speer, 1968; The JBHE Foundation, 2001).

CHAPTER 5

SCHOOL BOARD ZONE

The school board apparently did not expect the demand for desegregation, because it took them more than a month to come up with a legal response to the demand posed by Mrs. Brown and her associates. On May 17, 1948, at a special meeting, the school board passed a resolution dividing the town into two districts; they zoned one to the White community and the other to the Black community. The fact that Black and White children would pass each other's school when they went to their own school revealed the arbitrariness of the school zones (Katz & Tucker, Winter 1995/1996; Kaufman, 1989; Kluger, 2004; Speer, 1968; The JBHE Foundation, 2001).

However, Mrs. Brown and the NAACP had been preparing for all possible outcomes from their demands. Mrs. Brown talked to Dr. Davis, Rev. S. H. Lewis, Rev. Freeman and other NAACP officers in order to inform them of the humiliation and persecution she suffered at the dinner and thereafter. Then, they sought the advice of Attorney Towers who reluctantly assisted them because he was on the clock. He gave them advice on the condition that they pay him a legal fee of $250 (Brown, 1948c).

Attorney Towers said that the NAACP would win the case because the law was on their side. He promised that the South Park School would admit Black children in a month's time. Attorney Towers' indifference to the case was obvious; he was difficult to contact, and his lack of sincerity delayed the filing of the mandamus action for almost two months. It was only on May 25, 1948 that the case, *Webb v. School District No. 90*, was filed before the Kansas Supreme Court to compel the school district to admit Black students to the new South Park Common Grade School. The plaintiffs were the Walker School students (Brown, 1948c).

When Mrs. Brown apprised the NAACP of the delay and bickering that ensued at the Kansas City NAACP convention about the desegregation case, the national NAACP carefully studied the case and offered legal assistance (Dudley, 1948ac). Unlike southern states, Kansas did not have segregation laws on the books. Therefore, the NAACP saw this case as an "excellent opportunity to break down, once and for all, the segregation which has been arbitrarily in most instances practiced by local school boards" (Dudley, 1948b, p. 1). The only difficulty they foresaw was that the defendants would argue that they were not discriminating based on race because Black and White children just happened to attend separate schools, which, of course, was not true. The NAACP concluded that focusing on the unequal facilities between the two schools would not make the strongest argument and so they decided to argue that there were school children in both schools who lived in the other school zone and that the board created the school zones specifically to racially segregate the school children (Dudley, 1948b).

Mrs. Brown could not understand why a lawyer like Towers would charge such a high fee with the awareness that the local chapter of the NAACP was struggling to raise money for the case. Although she knew that lawyers had to earn their living, their case, in her mind, was a special one in which principles outweighed monetary benefits (Brown, 1948c). Mrs. Brown became impatient over procedural matters due to Towers' delays, and distrustful of the excessive monetary compensation he continuously requested. Mrs. Brown and the branch consequently lost confidence in Towers (Williams, 1948a). Mrs. Brown communicated all her misgivings about Towers to the NAACP headquarters in New York and succeeded in getting the help of another lawyer, Elisha Scott, to help move the case forward (Brown, 1948a; Scott, 1948).

On August 11, 1948, the NAACP officially retained Attorney Scott, a noted civil rights lawyer from Topeka, to replace Attorney Towers and the first thing Scott did was ask for a hearing on rescheduling the appointment with the commissioner to an earlier date. He then informed Mrs. Brown that the court would likely agree on the motion and consequently, they needed to pay a sum of $350 for the court fees by August 15, 1948 (Williams, 1948c). Since the branch lacked funds, Mrs. Brown raised $115 through various personal means and requested a loan from the national NAACP for the Kansas City chapter to take care of the balance. When the check did not arrive on time (Williams, 1948c), Mrs. Brown applied and received a personal loan at her bank without her husband's knowledge (Brown, 1948b). Mrs. Brown's personal commitment to the desegregation case in South Park included a number of financial contributions out of her own pocket to tide the local chapter over during the difficult times and this would turn out to be a regular feature of her activism.

Before Towers' resignation (Scott, 1948b), however, the school board in late July 1948 proposed a new deal in which they promised to improve Walker School and staff it with the best teachers available. The school board made what appeared to be a complete turnaround from the previous position they held. However, they did not anticipate the effect of the scare tactics they used against Mrs. Brown, so that rather than backtracking she was able to impress upon the NAACP Kansas City chapter the imperative of pursuing the case against segregation not only in Johnson County but in the whole state of Kansas. Compromise was certainly out of the picture when Mrs. Brown wrote optimistically that: "We are going to win this case [even] if it kills me, and then we are going to continue this action throughout the State" (Brown, 1948b, p. 2). The school board's scare tactics made Mrs. Brown more determined to see the fight for desegregation to the end. However, her fight would include not just the school board and their families but the NAACP and their families.

The national NAACP officials warily looked at Mrs. Brown's activities and initially characterized her negatively as the "one-woman show" and suggested that full NAACP cooperation should happen so the NAACP would have full control over the case (Marshall, 1948d). Sympathetic NAACP national officers like Mr. Franklin H. Williams, a noted New York civil rights lawyer, and Mr. Edward R. Dudley, another noted lawyer, defended Mrs. Brown; the former describing Mrs. Brown as "one of the few militant and outspoken members of the branch" (Williams, 1948d). When Mrs. Brown observed that the leadership of local chapters of the NAACP in Kansas

City, Kansas was a dismal failure, she had to take a leadership role in Merriam. As one of the leaders in the desegregation movement in South Park, Mrs. Brown was one of the first activists to stand up to the negative feedback from the Progressive Party, a left-wing political party that participated in the 1948 U.S. presidential election. They stated that the Kansas NAACP would lose the case, Mrs. Brown was the first positive voice in the sea of negative rhetoric to argue that the desegregation case would stimulate action in the NAACP branch to help fight segregation in a state where there were no Jim Crow laws but Blacks were being treated as if Jim Crow laws were on the books (Brown, 1948c). Mrs. Brown must have persuaded Charles Howard, a NAACP official and a Progressive Party member, because the NAACP decided to leave the case in the hands of the local leaders, including Mrs. Brown. Towers and others alleged that Mrs. Brown was only interested in the case for political reasons, mainly her affiliation with the Progressive Party (Brown, 1948c). Howard (1948) insisted that the national NAACP needed to take persuasive steps in moving the desegregation case out of the tight financial situation in which it had found itself. Therefore, Mrs. Brown felt she had to take a greater leadership role because she saw the financial and organizational needs, not because she wanted publicity and fame as suggested by some of her male counterparts in the NAACP.

In spite of the rejection by the Black community, the school board, after hearing arguments by the Merriam NAACP, started repairing the school by painting its walls inside and out, installing Venetian blinds on the windows, and sealing the basement to prevent flooding during the rainy season (Brown, 1948c).

In addition to the repairs of the school, the school board introduced another tactic, and submitted a motion to delay the hearing on the desegregation of South Park. The defendants postponed the meeting with the commissioner due to lack of preparation. The school board hired another attorney to assist their only lawyer. The Walker School principal started visiting the homes of the Black students to tell them that the board fixed their school, including providing new school books for the children. Sensing that these new school board developments might be divisive to the community and the movement, Mrs. Brown and her colleagues in the local NAACP branch spearheaded an educational campaign directed at the Black families who were wavering in order to prevent them from enrolling in the old Walker School (Brown, 1948c). Mrs. Brown proposed that the black students completely boycott the old school so that only one school would be available to accommodate both Black and White students. It was an equalization strategy designed to win the desegregation case, but it caused financial problems because Mrs. Brown needed to hire two private teachers and convince two NAACP members to use their homes as the temporary school sites while the case dragged on for several months. However, always the indefatigable fundraiser, Mrs. Brown afforded them additional funds to endure the school boycott.

CHAPTER 6

THE TRIAL BOYCOTT

Mrs. Brown strategically took advantage of the Black press so she received the needed publicity for the South Park desegregation case and the school boycott (Brown, 1948c). The state NAACP finally recognized Mrs. Brown's activism, and invited her to address the Kansas State Convention in September 1948 in Osawatomie, Kansas. Mrs. Brown shared her arguments against school segregation, appealed to the NAACP to make desegregation their top priority and called for the abolition of Jim Crow laws. Her message struck a chord among her listeners and following her address, the delegates gave a resounding vote of support for the South Park desegregation case. The press carried Mrs. Brown's statements against school segregation at the State Convention (Katz & Tucker, 1995), and the successful publicity campaign encouraged the people of Topeka to engage in a similar action to end segregation in their schools (Brown, 1948c).

With the opening of classes in September 1948, Walker School parents went to the new South Park School to enroll their children, only to be refused by the principal, who stated that he did not have the authority to enroll Black students while the court heard the desegregation case (Katz & Tucker, 1995). With the children, having been turned away, Mrs. Brown and the Merriam NAACP branch officers were resolved to completely abandon the Walker School. They talked to the Black parents and convinced them not to enroll at the old Walker School until they gave their testimonies before the commissioner (Brown, 1948e). The children testified at the court hearing about the inferior teachers they had and told the commissioner that they would never go back to the Walker School. The case united the Black community and others who were previously uninterested now joined the fight against segregation.

Mrs. Brown and the NAACP hired two excellent teachers to teach the children at two designated houses in Merriam, and they paid the teachers $100 a month. The chronic shortage of funds did not deter Mrs. Brown from pursuing the case. Instead, it pushed her to raise funds by contacting other NAACP branches in Kansas. As a result of her fundraising, Mrs. Brown discovered that the Kansas City branch had a monetary reserve, and she brought that finding to the attention of the national NAACP for a reallocation of the local funds to the case (Brown, 1948e).

While the financial situation of the desegregation case worried Mrs. Brown almost daily, she also had to contend with numerous telephone calls threatening to burn her house, calling her a "nigger lover," describing her as having "colored blood" in her veins and having a "black streak" on her back, and other name-calling attacks (Brown, 1948e). According to people opposed to the desegregation case, Mrs. Brown's so-called "communist agitation" had disturbed the community when previously all was at peace and in harmony (Brown, 1948e). The threats intensified when she invited her Black colleagues to eat lunch at her house on the day of the testimony, as her residence was close to the courthouse. On September 23, 1948, the Johnson County Herald reported on Mrs. Brown in the following unpalatable terms: "The sorest point with South Parkers, however, seems to be that a white advocate of mixed colored and white at the remodeled South Park School does not live in that school's district at all, and is sticking her nose in affairs which should be no concern of hers." However, this public persecution of Mrs. Brown actually became a rally call to the local NAACP branches (Brown, 1948d). In the city of Wichita, for example, the local NAACP branch became interested in supporting other desegregation cases (Williams, 1948e).

With the financial liability growing as the case continued, Attorney Williams of the NAACP Legal Department discussed with Attorney Scott the possibility of seeking a temporary injunction to force the school board to accept the Black school children into the South Park School pending the decision. Attorney Scott told him that the Kansas Supreme Court did not have jurisdiction over the case and suggested filing the temporary injunction at the local State District

Court with two additional plaintiffs. These two plaintiffs would be Black children who went to the South Park School to enroll. The NAACP instructed Attorney Scott to start the injunction proceedings a day after they appeared at the school (Williams, 1948e). It turned out, however, that Mr. Scott did not file the injunction because, according to Mrs. Brown (1948e), he was not able to get the additional fee of $100 he needed.

To address the problem of money needed to finance the litigation, Mrs. Brown called a luncheon meeting of NAACP officials in Kansas City in early October 1948 (Brown, 1948e). Mrs. Brown communicated to them that they needed to pay the salaries of the teachers at a cost of $200, plus Mr. Scott's legal fee, since he would not move on the case until he received his fee. In response, two women thought of baking cupcakes at 50 cents per dozen while Mrs. Brown took the responsibility of selling them. Mrs. Brown's extensive connections helped her deliver 125 dozens. They also sold enough tea with the cupcakes to raise an additional $50. Mrs. Brown was able to address the remaining balance by borrowing so she was able to pay the two teachers. The branch then asked for a $600 loan from the Kansas NAACP branch, and they agreed to loan $350 to pay Mr. Scott. Nevertheless, Scott was unable to get the injunction and the hearing was set for December 6, 1948. The commissioner compounded the financial problems for the desegregation case and school boycott by claiming to be ill so he could not attend the scheduled hearing.

Mrs. Brown was assiduous and ingenious with the brilliant ways in which she secured funding for the expenses of the desegregation case (Brown, 1948e). She broached the idea of collecting money from the NAACP with a letter from Dr. Davis, the state president of the Kansas NAACP authorizing the collection. Yet, after two months of follow-up, Dr. Davis did not act on it. Mrs. Brown providentially discovered that the NAACP branch in Kansas City had an inactive youth chapter. Mrs. Brown decided to work on rekindling the members of this chapter and inspired them to collect money for the segregation movement. When singer Billy Holiday came to the city in November 1948, the NAACP gave Mrs. Brown permission to appeal for donations ("Makes appeal for worthy cause," 1948). Mrs. Brown would add the money to the $45 available for the Black house teachers. Even though the weather was so bad that people stayed home, they were still able to raise $151 for the desegregation case (Brown, 1948f).

Mrs. Brown's close involvement with the local NAACP chapters in Kansas made her aware of the apathy of its officers and members. She came up with a plan to address the apathy. The branches had at least two meetings a month where approximately ten people attended. The members would pay their dues faithfully but the branch did nothing with their dues. They seemed to be ignorant of the mission of the NAACP, according to Mrs. Brown. The lack of activity of each NAACP chapter rendered these branches lifeless and ineffective. Mrs. Brown started showing the branches how to collect the money she needed for the desegregation case. Mrs. Brown also became critical about the way the national NAACP neglected and did not motivate the local branches (Brown, 1948e).

Mrs. Brown began to suspect that the hearing delays were deliberate, so she started to become distrustful of the current attorney, Mr. Scott. Mrs.

Brown's growing distrust of Mr. Scott was understandable because the delays increased their financial challenges. Raising money was not an easy task with the indifferent NAACP members and officers that she had to deal with almost daily. Her frustration with the delays was heightened when she received the news from Mr. Scott that the Supreme Court had received a request from the commissioner for the continuance of the case to March 1949 (Brown, 1948g; Scott, 1948c). Mrs. Brown was hoping for an emergency hearing but that was now out of the question (Brown, 1948f). In addition to the continuance, the two women who offered their homes as space for educating the children wanted to stop allowing this after December 6, 1948. Mrs. Brown shared all these concerns with Attorney Williams, including her suggestion of having a publicity man to create a greater awareness of the desegregation case to help her raise the needed money for the case.

The postponement of the hearing created enough dissatisfaction and lack of confidence that people were willing to give up the fight. The school board used every delay tactic they could to pressure the Black families to end their pursuit of justice. Some

Black families sent their children back to the old school. Mrs. Brown raised the concern that others would follow these parents and she could not blame them. To forestall this from happening, Mrs. Brown requested that Mr. Williams call Mr. Scott and tell him to act quickly on the injunction, and implored him to come down to Merriam and sort out the difficulties they were experiencing. The new legislature would exacerbate the challenging position that the local NAACP had with the case when they reconvened in January 1949, during which they would revise the statute that would have bearing on their case (Brown, 1948f).

As Mrs. Brown carried out a singular epistolary campaign for the case, she wrote letter after letter to persuade the national NAACP to take decisive remedial action on the impending crisis. The letters were so effective that Thurgood Marshall (1948b), the head of the NAACP legal department who questioned Mrs. Brown's leadership role, wired Mr. Scott telling him that delay was unthinkable, that swift action was imperative and that Mr. Scott must file the injunction or request a new commissioner immediately. Mr. Williams (1948f), at the same time, responded to Mrs. Brown's request to write a letter to the parents of the Black students stating that the NAACP appreciated all their heroic efforts, urging them not to give up and assuring them that the national NAACP will not abandon them at this critical hour. Williams (1948g, 1948h) also assisted Mrs. Brown with the publicity request by directing the head of the NAACP Public Relations Department to release a nationwide press release on the case with pictures of children, families and the school.

The letter from Mr. Williams had the intended effect of assuaging the fears and doubts of the parents and the members of the Merriam NAACP branch (Brown, 1948h). Mrs. Brown (1948i) also used the letter to stress that money would never be a problem again. When the two women requested to end the use of their houses as the temporary school, Mrs. Brown offered her house for the following week. When Mrs. Brown offered her own home, the two women agreed to extend the use of their houses for a few more days. During this time, with Mrs. Brown's two children sick in bed, she was unable to get out of the house to raise money for the two teachers who needed to be paid $135 each, plus $100 for an additional two weeks

(Brown, 1948i). Even with the financial challenges of the temporary school, Mrs. Brown continued pushing forward with the desegregation case.

Mr. Scott, unhappy with the order from Mr. Marshall to move forward with the case, reluctantly filed for an injunction and asked for an additional $15 fee. However, the judge again delayed the case because he wanted to confer with the county attorney who happened to be representing the school board. Mrs. Brown felt that this incidental information might mean that Mr. Scott would never get the injunction, which proved to be correct when, on December 16, the lower court denied the petition ("Press release," 1948; "Petition fails," 1948). The lower court did not agree with the argument that an emergency existed to warrant the issuance of a temporary injunction given that a school, the Walker School, was available to the petitioners. Pending the decision of the higher court on the mandamus action, the judge declared that the court did not have jurisdiction over the petition (Brown, 1948j). With this judgment, the judge dashed any hope that an injunction would force the South Park School to accommodate the Black students and ease the financial burden of supporting these students with their private classes. Mrs. Brown correctly expected the lower court not to grant a temporary injunction, and the adverse decision would aggravate the financial burden that the Merriam NAACP branch already felt (Williams, 1948i).

Unfortunately, the news of the denial took the Black community's spirit to an all-time low (Brown, 1948j). They were also quickly losing their trust in Attorney Scott who had told them that he could get the temporary injunction and emergency hearing, which did not happen. Mrs. Brown finally realized, after the delay tactics and eventual decision of the court that the people behind the scenes were really against them and were on the side of the school board from the beginning.

Then suddenly, the commissioner wanted to meet Mr. Scott and the lawyer for the school board so that he could ask for an emergency hearing, a puzzling action that revealed and confirmed that the commissioner was working for the other side. The decision by the court in favor of the South Park School motivated the school board to ask for an earlier verdict on the mandamus action. Mr. Scott became so anxious that he requested assistance with the case. The Merriam NAACP branch wanted the national NAACP to send someone to Merriam who could provide guidance for the next course of action. In the midst of this debacle, a local church in the community finally agreed to house the temporary school for the Black children. The community still needed to provide payment of $250 for the teachers and for maintenance of the church facilities so Mrs. Brown requested a loan from the national NAACP, arguing that repayment was not a problem because she was able to raise the money for the repayment of the last loan.

The negative ruling prompted the state NAACP in Kansas to convene a state board meeting, which resulted in a "brawl" (Brown, 1948k, p.1). Dr. Davis, the state NAACP president, presided over the meeting. Unfortunately, he spent the majority of the meeting time talking about his work until Mrs. Brown confronted him about financially supporting the desegregation case. Mrs. Brown became furious when Dr. Davis said that the Merriam case was not the concern of the state NAACP because it was only a local community problem. Although furious at that statement, Mrs. Brown still communicated her needs at the board meeting.

Mrs. Brown stated that she needed financial support for the compensation of the temporary school teachers. She stated that they had only received $600 from the Kansas City branch of the NAACP and nothing from the state NAACP. It turned out that Dr. Davis had made a private deal with the Kansas City branch to give the $600 to the Merriam school case to free the branch from participating in another segregation case in Wichita, Kansas, and Dr. Davis wanted the branch to give the impression that this money came from the state NAACP, not from the Kansas City branch. Dr. Davis also took issue with Mrs. Brown's correspondences with the national NAACP, saying that she had no business communicating with the national office. Dr. Davis saw Mrs. Brown's solid commitment to fight segregation as a threat to his influence in Kansas as the state president of the NAACP (Brown, 1948k).

In response to Mrs. Brown's request for additional support, the national NAACP suggested that the state NAACP sponsor a car raffle. The suggestion did not rest well with the state NAACP members, so it did not pass at the state board meeting. In the reading of the minutes, however, the secretary read that it passed and they wanted Mrs. Brown and the head of the steering committee to work on it. Both refused because they knew it was voted down and felt people would be lukewarm to the raffle. In protest, the head of the steering committee resigned. The president did not propose an alternative, so the state NAACP left the question of funding unanswered (Brown, 1948k).

The board meeting also tackled the status of another desegregation case developing in Wichita (Brown, 1948k). In early October 1948, the Executive Committee members of the Kansas State Conference and representatives of Wichita, Topeka and Merriam gathered and agreed unanimously to file a lawsuit challenging the legality of segregation in Wichita (Williams, 1949b). In November 1948, Carrie L. Burney sent a letter to a Black daily paper that put in question the Topeka desegregation case. Furthermore, the case was in shambles as confusion arose when the teachers accused the NAACP of trying to replace the "Negro" teachers (Brown, 1948k, p. 2). Mrs. Brown argued that any action was premature, as the state NAACP had not studied the Wichita case seriously, had not yet informed the teachers involved about the facts, and did not know the proper course of action. Dr. Davis received a letter from one of the teachers involved asking about the state NAACP's plan of action. The state president responded later by stating he would visit Wichita to discuss the issues. Rumor had it that teachers were signing up for NAACP membership for the ostensible purpose of defeating a plan of action in favor of the Wichita case. The Wichita branch voted Carrie L. Burney into office in December 1948 as a member of the Executive Committee of the Wichita branch (Williams, 1949b). The complaint of their White lawyer caused further difficulties for the Wichita case because he began asking for compensation even though at the time he took the case he stated that he was not interested in any fees (Brown, 1948k). The state NAACP's internal and external struggles made Mrs. Brown's work to desegregate public education more challenging, but she persevered through the opponents of desegregation inside and outside the NAACP.

Mrs. Brown was a formidable pillar of strength in the midst of the difficulties. While others were more interested in fame and honor than working together to defeat segregation, she had put her mind and resources to the case. However, it seemed that many did not understand her hard work. Mrs. Brown stated in a letter to Mr. Williams, "This case is always on my mind and frankly I can't think about anything else and of course the people won't let me. I will do anything for these folks out here who have tried so hard, and it breaks my heart every time they are disappointed. I feel they have been somewhat victimized by attorneys, ignorance, lack of cooperation etc., and none of us can stand much more" (1948k, p. 4). Mrs. Brown did not want to fail the children of South Park and this commitment to be a woman of her word weighed on her heavily night and day as she faced many relentless legal and personal challenges to desegregation in public education in South Park.

Sympathetic to Mrs. Brown's suggestions, including her appeal to send someone to help Mr. Scott and write a letter to Mr. Freeman, Kansas City NAACP chapter president, Mr. Williams (1948j, 1948k) took several steps during the third week of December. First, he contacted Mr. Carl R. Johnson, president of the NAACP's Kansas City, Missouri branch, for the letter to go to Topeka and see Mr. Scott, examined the case and advised on the necessary course of action (Williams, 1948j). Prior to meeting Mr. Scott, Johnson had to first see Mrs. Brown to get the whole picture. Financial constraints and lack of personnel prevented the national NAACP office from sending someone immediately to Merriam. Mr. Johnson was seen as the advance party to ascertain the strength and merit of the case and help the national office decide on the next move to expedite the lawsuit (Williams, 1948l). Upon Mr. Williams' receipt of the letter (1948l), Mrs. Brown traveled all the way to her home state in Kansas City, Missouri and apprised Mr. Johnson on the case. After being briefed on the case, the latter concluded that the case handling "smells a little" (Johnson, 1948a, p. 1). Mr. Williams also wrote a letter to Mr. Freeman acknowledging the Kansas City branch donation of $600 and appreciating their support, both financial and moral (Williams, 1948k). He also sent a letter to Dr. Davis inquiring on the status of the case; the letter he received as a reply alluded to Mrs. Brown's unwanted meddling in the case when he wrote that: "everyone tries to run the show, and step back for us to pay the bill" (Davis, 1948, p.1). This statement by Dr. Davis demonstrates the continuous blatant and subtle political struggle within the movement faced by Mrs. Brown on a daily basis for leadership and recognition by her colleagues in the desegregation of public education in South Park.

The perennial problem of funding concerning the salaries of the two teachers for the temporary school gave Mrs. Brown the impetus (1948l) to gauge whether these different NAACP branches were willing to help. She learned that some branches wanted to help financially in support of the private classes for the Black school children but felt the national NAACP office would disapprove of this type of support. She asked for an opinion from the national office on the possibility of collecting contributions from these branches. Mr. Williams (1949a) agreed that collecting contributions from them was legally permissible under the present circumstances. In her desperation to get the $200 to pay the teachers, Mrs. Brown went to see Mr. Johnson to ask for a loan from the Kansas City branch, which coincided with the directive from Mr. Williams that Mr. Johnson should first see Mrs. Brown. Given the financial straits the branch was in, Mr. Johnson promised that his branch would vote in support of financially supporting the desegregation case. However, unable to get the needed money, Mrs. Brown made a personal loan of $200 and raised $30 on the same day. Mrs. Brown believed that staying out of the "Jim Crow" school was the best course of action as they waited for the decision of the court, and it was in agreement with the position of the national NAACP (Williams, 1949a). As of January 10, 1949, legal fees and expenses related to the private education of the Black students had amounted to $1726.02 with $1076.02 paid for the litigation and the rest for teachers' salaries from October 1948 to December 1948, and the expenses of the rental of chairs and tables from September 1948 to December 1948. The total did not include incidental expenses such as phone calls, traveling expenses, stamps, mail, coal, and utilities, which amounted to about $120, most of which had been paid from the pocket of Mrs. Brown ("Expenditures in the Merriam Kansas School Case," 1949).

In early January, Mr. Johnson talked to Mr. Scott and concluded that the case was "in good shape" (Brown, 1949a, p. 1). Although such was the case, the commissioner again delayed in submitting the report to the Kansas Supreme Court, blaming the delay on the weather. All these delays were deliberate, but instead of becoming discouraged, these delays hardened Mrs. Brown's resolve not to return to the "Jim Crow" school. The school board took advantage of the delay when several Black parents and their children defected to their side. These defectors were now trying to convince those who held out that it was futile to fight segregation. These defectors told the other parents that they would end up coming back to the old Walker School and that it was better to give up and save their money then to continue with the pointless struggle. The school board also did not waste time in bribing the Black children to return by offering to provide free lunches. The board also told the two teachers to tell the Black children that the fight to desegregate was foolish. In response to this negative propaganda, the two private teachers hired by Merriam NAACP branch started visiting the homes of the Black students who went back to the Walker School and succeeded in convincing ten pupils to return to the temporary school, to the delight of Mrs. Brown.

Mrs. Brown was constantly in search of ways to raise money (Brown, 1949a). She was able to raise $175 for the loan she borrowed from the bank. But as the teachers' salaries had to be paid, she needed to do some more fundraising activities. Having received an affirmative response to her plan by the national NAACP to raise money, Mrs. Brown wrote all the branches asking for monetary contributions with a letter from the national office legitimizing the fund drive. The Topeka branch president did not want to give any financial support because the state president, Dr. Davis, did not approve of the temporary school. This did not sit well with Mrs. Brown, who called the branch three times and organized a challenge at their regular meeting. As a result of her advocacy, Mrs. Brown was able to get $75 from the Topeka branch. Mr. Johnson, on the other hand, pledged $100 from the Kansas City, Missouri branch (Brown, 1949a). Mrs.

Brown also publicized the details of Mr. Williams' letter in The Call. The Wichita branch members who had an election that voted into office those who were against the fight to end segregation in schools in that area initially wanted to convey that no money would come from them; yet members made a motion to collect money and received $22 (Wetmore, 1949). All of Mrs. Brown's activities were accomplished singlehandedly, in spite of the fact that she could not leave her home for long periods of time because of her domestic responsibilities, as she no longer had a maid (Brown, 1949a).

However, one of the casualties of her domestic responsibilities as a wife and mother of two young daughters was her ability to send pictures documenting the desegregation movement in Kansas. Mrs. Brown was unable to send photos to the national NAACP until the following year, in January 1949. Nevertheless, the national office in an effort to raise money for the teachers by creating awareness of the case was able to publish an article in The Crisis without the requested photographs (Williams, 1949c). When Mrs. Brown tried to remedy this request for pictures, she learned that the photographer had lost the negatives. Luckily, Mr. Scott had duplicates of the pictures but kept forgetting to send them. Even with the responsibilities that come with taking care of her two children and home, Mrs. Brown did everything she could to get the money needed for the salaries of the two temporary school teachers (Brown, 1949b).

In his report to the national NAACP office, Mr. Johnson (1949a) explained that those who do not understand the legal procedure may not understand that delay is the natural course in litigation. Mr. Johnson sided with Mr. Scott and blamed the commissioner for the delay in the case. Having examined the pleadings and brief, Mr. Johnson held the opinion that the case should be argued on the basis that the state of Kansas, with the exception of first-class cities, does not provide for segregation in schools, rather than on references to unequal facilities. Upon reading the actual report by the commissioner, Mr. Johnson concluded that the petitioners should drop the argument for equal facilities because of the commissioner's avoidance of the sufficient evidence to conclude that the separate school was in violation of the law (Johnson, 1949b). Mr.

Johnson's conclusion agreed with the separate opinion of Mr. Marshall (1949a).

While the commissioner made his report available to both parties in the case, the commissioner again delayed filing (Brown, 1949c). He said that he would submit it no later than January 25, but it took several more days for the commissioner to file it in court (Brown, 1949d). Naturally, Mrs. Brown was upset because it was prolonging her never ending task of securing money for the temporary school teachers. During that month, she was able to collect $227 and extend her personal loan for 60 additional days. She concurred with Mr. Johnson that the report was preparing the groundwork to have equal but separate schools. Although she liked receiving praise in the review of the case, Mrs. Brown did not agree that the delay had to do only with the procedure and not to Mr. Scott's delaying tactics, which appeared to coincide with the commissioner's. Mrs. Brown would never fully trust Mr. Scott.

The NAACP finally granted the request from the Merriam branch to send someone to help Mr. Scott with the desegregation case when Mr. Williams agreed to assist Mr. Scott himself (Carter, 1949; Marshall, 1949a; Williams, 1949d, 1949e). Mr. Scott (1949a) had already requested personally that Mr. Williams assist him in the argument. The delay in the filing of the report postponed Mr. William's trip to Kansas so that Scott (1949b) asked again for Mr. Williams' assistance, a request that Mr. Marshall approved earlier and authorized again (Williams, 1949f). When the commissioner finally filed the report, Mr. Scott filed two motions: one was to advance the hearing from March to an earlier date and the other was to take exception to certain conclusions in the commissioner's report (Brown, 1949d). On the first motion, however, the Kansas Supreme Court turned him down.

Mrs. Brown took it as her duty to present the commission's report to the Merriam branch's executive committee (1949d). Members expressed their disappointment that the report gave them the feeling that they could not get a favorable ruling from the Kansas Supreme Court. Instead of being discouraged and settling for the separate but equal doctrine as Mrs. Brown had feared, the executive committee was talking about elevating the case to the U.S. Supreme Court (Brown, 1949d).

Publicity paid off when a letter from a New Yorker who had read the Crisis article and wrote to express moral support arrived at the Merriam NAACP branch (Brown, 1949d). The letter, which the branch members read enthusiastically, boosted the low morale of the branch. Finally, in February, Mrs. Brown sent the photographs, promising more pictures on the way. She encouraged them to use the pictures immediately to solicit the money they needed. In fact, she replied to the New York letter from E. Snell Hall asking for a monetary donation. Mr. Hall obliged by sending a $100 check and stated that he was going to ask the national NAACP office to forward his contribution of $500 or part of it to the Merriam branch. Mrs. Brown was overjoyed with the contribution because she was making sure the NAACP paid the teachers. She asked the national NAACP office whether they could "divert" the money from Mr. Hall to them as per his request.

The condition at the temporary school grounds was heartbreaking to Mrs. Brown (Brown, 1949d). Mrs. Brown, the primary strategist behind this plan of action, recognized how difficult the situation had become for the teachers and students. The teachers had to fire up the church furnace in the cold weather, so the children had no choice but to inhale the noxious smoke. They had no books. All eight grades gathered in one room and the teachers would tutor pupils individually throughout the day. But the school children were unwavering in their desire to stay away from the old Walker School and wait for the decision that would enable them to enter the new South Park School. When one teacher became sick, Mrs. Brown taught the first, second, third and fourth grades without hesitation. As a result of teaching, Mrs. Brown became aware of the awful conditions the teachers and students experienced. Therefore, Mrs. Brown was the most apprehensive about the court delays, because she knew firsthand the poor situation the teachers and pupils experienced at the temporary school. Adding to growing concerns about the condition of the temporary school was the news that in March, the school board planned a meeting to elect new members of the board, receive complaints and accept submissions for the teachers' contracts.

The date for the argument before the Kansas Supreme Court was finally set on March 1, 1949 (Scott, 1949c). Weeks prior to the hearing, the Wichita Committee on Racial Equality broached the idea of submitting an amicus curiae brief in support of the Merriam case (Holmes, 1949; Williams, 1949g). Williams, who was instructed and authorized to be present at the argument, received a telegram from Scott (1949d) on February 25, 1949 stating that the defendant's motion for a continuance was approved and the court postponed the hearing again to April 5, 1949. The continuance, however, did not prevent Mr. Williams from going to Topeka to confer with Mr. Scott regarding the case.

While preparing to go to the hearing, Williams (1949h), who seemed to have expected the approval of the continuance, continued to contact people and publications that could publicize the case. Having received the photographs, he urged Mrs. Brown to send him personal details concerning the families in the photos, their income, their suffering, and their efforts to raise money. He was able to contact Will Maslow, director of the Commission on Law and Action of the

American Jewish Congress who in turn contacted Mr. Sidney Lawrence, head of the Community Relations Bureau of the Jewish Federation and Council of Greater Kansas City. Mr. Williams (1949i) wanted Mrs. Brown to get in touch with Mr. Lawrence to explain to him the background of the case in hopes it would lead to financial or legal assistance. Mrs. Brown immediately did this, and even arranged for two agencies to submit amicus briefs in support of the Merriam case (Johnson, 1949c). Mr. Williams (1949k) also co-authored a story on the case and sent it to The New Republic and The Nation with the latter making an editorial note on the issue.

Mr. Scott (1949e) feared that the judge would grant a continuance again, so he appeared before the chief justice of the Kansas Supreme Court to register the plaintiffs' opposition to any further continuances. Mr. Williams could understand a second continuance but a third seemed to be excessive so he believed that "the decision in this case has been too long delayed as it is," a conviction Mrs. Brown had maintained (Williams, 1949j, p. 1). Mrs. Brown's conviction proved to be correct. The Supreme Court did not grant another continuance so on April 5, 1949 Mr. Scott and Mr. Williams argued the case for the desegregation of the all-white public school, South Park School.

CHAPTER 7

THE COURT DECISION

Attorneys Scott and Williams, traveling from New York, argued the case before the Kansas Supreme Court, maintaining that South Park school board's zoning lines were arbitrarily drawn to segregate Black school children who were attending the dilapidated Walker School, which was a violation of existing laws (Williams, 1949l). The attorney for the South Park school board, Casey Jones, admitted before the court that the zoning lines were created arbitrarily so that both White and Black school children would pass their respective schools. Mr. Williams received commendations from the national NAACP and the Merriam NAACP for his "splendid" performance

(Howard, 1949). Mr. Scott praised Mr. Williams' presentation as having "made a wonderful impression before the court and the spectators" (Howard, 1949, p. 1).

Mrs. Brown excitedly expected a favorable decision after the hearing. In addition to seeing the fruit of her activism, a favorable decision would free her from her almost daily fundraising activities. In the meantime, however, Mrs. Brown was still as busy as ever traveling throughout Kansas to raise more money for the case. The case was wearing her out although she was "just as interested and determined to help clean this situation in this state" (Brown, 1949e, p.1). Her personal expenses for the cause totaled approximately $1035 from April 1948 to May 1949. However, those personal expenses did not include her contributions to the NAACP branch, payment of school utilities, coal expenses, table rentals and teachers' salaries. The actual amount of her contributions will never be known because she did not keep a record. Mrs. Brown never expected to be reimbursed because she saw herself as a volunteer ("Financial statement,"

1949, p. 3). Mrs. Brown would continue to raise money for the case up to the day of the final decision.

During the trial, the South Park school board elected new directors. The new school board continued using their tactics of intimidation to frighten the Black community and sow seeds of division (Brown, 1949e). The school board said that the integration of White and Black school children would never be acceptable and they would use every means possible to prevent it. Property owners feared that real estate prices would go down once the Black children were admitted to the South Park School. In response to community fears, the South Park school board passed a tax levy to finance improvements at the Walker School (Brown, 1949f; Williams, 1949m, 1949n). Mrs. Brown proposed that the NAACP should fight the tax levy in the courts (Williams, 1949m). Mr. Williams (1949m) stated that a tax levy fight would be too expensive but agreed that some type of campaign should be organized to put an end to the school board's strategy. Mr. Williams (1949n) also discussed whether the school board could circumvent the law by improving the Walker School after their anticipated favorable decision in *Webb*.

While waiting for the final verdict, Mrs. Brown (1949e; 1949f) used the time to raise money for the case and presided over the Black students' graduation ceremony from their NAACP-supported school (Williams, 1949n; Brown, 1949h). During this time of fundraising, the Federated Negro Women's Club in Kansas City, Missouri invited Mrs. Brown to speak to a group in Newton, Kansas who raised $60.65 for the case. The American Legion Group and the Negro Business Men's Club in Topeka also invited Mrs. Brown to speak, and they raised $46.50 for the case (Brown, 1949h). In Manhattan, Kansas, she spoke before the Manhattan Civil Rights Committee, enlightening the audience on the status of the case and the sacrifices of parents who had to send their children to private tutors (Brown, 1949f; 1949g; "Manhattan," 1949). As a result, she was able to raise $123. In her meeting with the Civil Rights Committee members, who were opposed to fighting segregation akin to the Wichita case, Mrs. Brown realized that the lack of information on desegregation was the main reason they opposed the campaign to end segregation. It was only when they were informed about the facts in the South

Park case that their antagonism vanished and they were willing to help with both the case and the desegregation movement.

In a report to Mr. White, the overall financial contributions that the Merriam NAACP raised for the South Park case excluding Mrs. Brown's expenses amounted to approximately $3000 (Brown, 1949e). Mrs. Brown was able to get the Merriam NAACP to agree that if they raised more money than they needed for the South Park case, the balance would be used to fight segregation statewide. She also discussed the possibility of using the extra money for NAACP memberships and subscriptions to the NAACP magazine, The Crisis.

By June, the school board had finished extensive repairs to the Walker School (Brown, 1949h). South Park teachers started inviting people from Kansas City, Missouri to belie the accusations of bad facilities and to publicize that the campaign against segregation was actually being used for other purposes. At the same time, within the state NAACP, an internal problem arose when Dr. Davis told the Wichita NAACP not to let Mrs. Brown come and collect money for the South Park case (1949i). Having learned of this betrayal, Mrs. Brown became angry. Pretending to be ignorant of all of Mrs. Brown's sacrifices, Dr. Davis systematically began to sow seeds of discord statewide. Mrs. Brown implored the national NAACP to write to Mr. Bettis, president of the Wichita NAACP, and Mr. Dunbar Reed, an official at the same branch, to advise them on Dr. Davis' actions.

Finally, on June 11, 1949, the Kansas Supreme Court released its decision on the desegregation case. The Supreme Court ordered the Johnson School District to accept Black students into the South Park School that coming school year. Mrs. Brown and the Merriam residents were ecstatic with the decision (Brown, 1949j).

The next step of implementation, however, was rather difficult. The community needed to prepare to accept integration, and work to prevent race riots similar to ones that happened in St. Louis, Missouri and Youngstown, Ohio following the decision to allow integrated swimming pools there (Lawrence, 1949). The national NAACP, through Mr. Williams (1949p), recognized this need upon receiving a copy of a letter from Mrs. Brown coming from Mr. Sidney Laurence, director of the community relations bureau of the Jewish Federation and Council of Greater Kansas City, in Missouri. He suggested carrying out an educational program in South Park "to assure a smooth effectuation of the judicial order in this case" would be advisable (Williams, 1949p, p.1).

The South Park school board did not accept the decision of the Kansas Supreme Court, and this came as no surprise to Mrs. Brown. The school board told the Merriam people that they would overturn the decision (Brown, 1949j). The school board also continued relentlessly with the repairs to the Walker School. The school board employed Black people to invite the Black South Park parents to a meeting following the court decision to talk about the $8000 from the tax levy now designated to the construction of a new kindergarten for Black students. They stated that all students would attend the South Park School except the school children who would be attending the new kindergarten at the Walker School. There was also a plan for the school board to circulate a petition stating that Blacks wanted to attend the Walker School. Mrs. Brown saw right through their strategy to maintain segregated schools. Mrs. Brown believed that the school board would send some White students to the Walker School for a brief period, only to meet the desegregation order. At the school board meeting on the new kindergarten, the board required 51 percent of the Black residents in South Park to sign a petition demanding the board not to tear down the Walker School before they would agree to allocate $8000 for the construction of the new kindergarten (Brown, 1949k). Mrs. Brown confronted all these attempts to circumvent the court order to desegregate the schools in South Park.

The national NAACP, however, believed that there was no problem with the plan to improve the Walker School since the decision mandated the rezoning of the district on a reasonable basis (Williams, 1949q). There was no harm from the tax levy because the repair of the Walker School would guarantee equal facilities for both Black and White students. Therefore, a taxpayers' suit was not necessary, according to the national NAACP. The Kansas Supreme Court retained jurisdiction over the matter so that the school board's noncompliance could be grounds for a motion for contempt. The national NAACP shifted their attention to a statewide desegregation movement.

In preparation for the statewide fight against segregation in Kansas, the national NAACP office prepared a questionnaire to ascertain the status and conditions of segregation statewide (Williams, 1949o). Dr. Davis, however, stalled the implementation (Brown, 1949j). When Mrs. Brown heard about Dr. Davis' delay tactic, she asked for 30 to 35 copies so that she could deliver them.

By late July, the homeowners' association put a twist in the plan to repair the school (Brown, 1949l). The association circulated a petition stating that all Black residents wanted to maintain the Walker School so that their children could attend. The school board used a Black religious man to defend the petition. The school board even asked the Supreme Court clerk about the petition, and the clerk said that they could maintain the Walker School and those who wanted to attend the Walker School could do it voluntarily. There was a group of Black residents who wanted a segregated school. The school board knew this, and focused their efforts on this particular group of Black segregationists.

Mrs. Brown (1949l), who now knew the people in Merriam, disagreed with Mr. Franklin on the seemingly harmless idea behind the improvement of the Walker School. Considering the small size of the community, she felt the maintenance of two schools was impractical. Mrs. Brown understood that the repairs on the Walker School were made only to maintain segregation at all costs. The hope for the establishment of two unsegregated schools in South Park was not wishful thinking, according to Mrs. Brown, since the White residents in South Park would never send their children to Walker School. Mrs. Brown believed that by exposing legally the shenanigans of the South Park school board, like their refusal to audit their books, closed board meetings, and the illegal coercion of people to sign petitions, the NAACP could discourage the school board from pursuing the plan of renovating the Walker School. Mrs. Brown believed that legal action should be taken because "[i]f the Walker School is maintained this Sept. we have not had a victory regardless of what the Supreme Court says. There is no reason for maintaining [sic] the Walker

School and I think we should do all in our power to prevent its use" (Brown, 1949l, p.2).

Mrs. Brown resented being labeled "hysterical" because of her stance after the decision of the Kansas Supreme Court. Mrs. Brown stated that she was only a "realist" and honestly believed that if the Black community was left alone and without her leadership "95% of them will attend the Walker School, because they are sick and tired of all the abuse, uncertainty [sic], conflicting ideas, Elisha Scott, etc." (Brown, 1949l, p.2). Mrs. Brown stated, "But so far, I am the only one who has given everything, not even the people in South Park, would sacrifice the things I have, and when things do not go right, I am the only one who will do anything about it – there is no one else" (Brown, 1949l, p.2).

At this critical juncture in the desegregation of education in South Park, Mrs. Brown bore the brunt of the relentless persecution coming from the school board. The school board incited the community into a campaign of hate against her. She was labeled a "communist," and described as having bad morals because she was associating with Black residents, and accused of stealing money, among other things.

(Brown, 1948l, p. 3). When Mrs. Brown reached out to the new members of the school board, they told her that the White community hated her more than anyone in the Black community. They told her that she was the reason why the Black children would not have a school to attend in the coming academic year because she stole the money. They also told her that she was the prime agitator in the Black community and the chief instigator in the legal proceedings. They stated that the community could have reached a compromise if she had not been involved (Brown, 1948l, p.4).

In the midst of this challenging moment as a leader in this movement, Mrs. Brown remained optimistic despite the relentless persecution by the South Park school board. The inactivity of the state NAACP and the apathy of the Black community made her activism even more challenging but she stayed focused on the goal to desegregate education in South Park and persevered.

Mrs. Brown discovered that more money could be raised for the desegregation movement following the decision in the South Park case. The verdict stirred up people to contribute more money. Following the decision of the South Park case, many churches and organizations invited Mrs. Brown to speak about the desegregation case and movement. Although Mrs. Brown told them that she was not asking for donations, many insisted on giving money to the NAACP. Mrs. Brown continued to receive letter after letter stating that people were willing to contribute money to the desegregation movement if needed. Mrs. Brown replied to these letters by sending articles on the decision of the case and thanking them. As a result of this support, Mrs. Brown and the Merriam NAACP were able to pay the $235 they owed to the national NAACP.

In the early weeks of August, the Homeowners Association submitted petitions to the school board stating that the Black families who signed did not want to attend the South Park School, and that they were satisfied with the Walker School, provided it was repaired. The school board then submitted a motion to the Supreme Court requesting that the Walker School be maintained and attendance be made voluntarily. The school board then stated that $4,000 would be allotted for the construction of inside toilets, another classroom, a telephone and the hiring of another teacher in addition to the two existing teachers (Brown, 1949m,1949o). Most of the Black families signed the petition, because they were told that Walker School would be turned into a school playground. Mrs. Brown (1949m) recognized the school board's strategy to maintain the segregated school for Black students with the deceptive help of the Homeowners' Association. In the midst of their strategy of deception, the school board voluntarily started the repairs on the Walker School.

Upon reading the school board's motion, Mr. Scott suggested that the Merriam people gather a delegation to see the Chief Justice in Topeka. The interview did not go well and it dawned on Mrs. Brown that Mr. Scott did not know what to do. It was only when Mr. Howard was contacted that Mr. Scott agreed to file a protest. Mrs. Brown called for a taxpayers' lawsuit. She believed that it would be the best way to counter the school board's illegal activities. When asked about whether he would assist, Mr. Scott asked for a fee of $250. Having gotten in touch with Mr. Laurence Holmes, who had interest in taking over the injunction suit with Mr. Howard, and Mr. Johnson agreeing to work with the case, Mrs. Brown and the branch agreed to release Mr. Scott although he later said that the motion had been drawn, which Mrs. Brown did not believe to be true.

One good consequence of the decision was that in mid-August five black students from South Park were accepted for enrollment at the Shawnee Mission High School, which catered only to White students (Brown, 1949n). To maintain segregation, this high school paid the tuition and transportation of black students to Sumner and Northeast Jr. When the parents of the remaining three or four black students were told that they had to pay for their tuition and transportation to the so-called "Jim Crow" high school, they immediately agreed to enroll at Shawnee Mission. This piece of good news, however, was overshadowed by the decision of the Supreme Court granting the motion by the school board since it went unopposed. The necessity of filing the injunction suit was heightened by this action and as a result, Mr. Holmes and Mr. Johnson met to work on it although the national NAACP and Mr. Carter believed that taxpayers' suit "should be avoided whenever possible because it is most difficult to maintain" (Brown, 1949b, p.1).

To counteract the granted motion, Mrs. Brown and her allies earnestly tried to unify the Black residents and get them to attend the South Park School. There is no doubt that Mrs. Brown used all her capabilities and connections to convince the branch members of the cause and to persuade them to convince others to do the same. Speakers from the NAACP were invited to strongly encourage the Black students to attend only the South Park School. The NAACP circulated petitions to get signatures of those who were bent on attending the South Park School while the school board circulated their petition for the Walker School. Then, on September 7th, the school board announced a notice of meeting for "patrons" of the Walker School. Only two representatives from the branch went to the meeting, which was also attended by two Blacks and three school board members. The letter said that the Supreme Court agreed to let them build a $60,000 Walker School with $5000 allotted for each year to be completed on the twelfth year. The branch members, however, said that the money would go to waste as the

Black children would go to South Park School, not to Walker School. The school board said that the construction would continue.

Then, on September 9, 1949, the day of reckoning arrived: the date for school registration. Every Black student enrolled at the South Park School. The Walker School opened for two and a half days with not a single student coming to register. Mrs. Brown called it "a tremendous victory." The sacrifices and hardships were all worth it according to Mrs. Brown (Brown, 1949o, p. 2).

CHAPTER 8

SCHOOL DISTRICT NO. 90

On May 1, 1949, Mrs. Brown's relentless local activism led to the successful outcome of her South Park desegregation case, *Webb v. School District No. 90*, in which the Supreme Court of Kansas ordered the school district of Merriam to integrate their all-white South Park School by the beginning of the new academic term in September 1949. Mrs. Brown did not stop with the success of *Webb v. School District No. 90*. She wanted to desegregate public schools across the state of Kansas so she started working with the Topeka NAACP branch. In Topeka, Mrs. Brown helped to identify potential plaintiffs in a case challenging Topeka's racially segregated school system. She identified Oliver Brown, a railroad welder and minister, who became the plaintiff on behalf of his daughter, Linda Brown, for what would become the landmark desegregation case, *Brown v. Board of Education* (1954). Mrs. Brown also lobbied the NAACP's Legal Defense Fund to help with the litigation of the Brown case. In 1954, the decision of this landmark case outlawed racial segregation in all public schools across the nation. The secretary of the Topeka NAACP, Lucinda Todd, believed the landmark civil rights case occurred because of Mrs. Brown's leadership. (Katz & Tucker, Winter 1995/1996; Kaufman, 1989; Kluger, 2004; Speer, 1968; The JBHE Foundation,2001).

CHAPTER 9
THE UNSUNG HEROINE

Introduction

Mrs. Esther Brown, a White Jewish woman from a Russian family of immigrants who identified with the disenfranchisement of the Black community in Merriam, Kansas, became an unsung Black feminist ally of the desegregation movement of the 1940s and 1950s in America. She sacrificed much for this movement, including her own marriage. Mrs. Brown's fearless feminist activities relegated her to a place of invisibility in the contemporary public narrative on desegregation in public education in Merriam, Kansas by the Black male leadership of the NAACP in the 1940s and 1950s (Barnett, 1993). For example, Thurgood Marshall, director of the NAACP legal department, characterized

Mrs. Brown's leadership in the desegregation movement in Merriam, Kansas as a "one woman show," along with a follow up statement that the NAACP did not want her to serve as the face of this potentially successful desegregation campaign in public education, so he strongly encouraged his male NAACP colleagues to get involved in the litigation process (Marshall, 1948d). However, the NAACP continued to work with Mrs. Brown, because it quickly became clear that she understood the equalization strategy designed to desegregate public education and she had relentless passion.

Birthing of the Activist

Who was Mrs. Esther Brown? Mrs. Brown, a suburban American-born Jewish housewife and mother of two young daughters from Merriam, Kansas, challenged racial segregation in public education in her school district beginning in the late 1940s. Mrs. Brown's social consciousness and activism started as a young girl in her working-class immigrant neighborhood in Kansas City, Missouri and continued throughout her life.

Mrs. Brown's father, Ben Swirk, raised her by himself after the death of her mother. Her father was a member of several left-wing labor organizations including the International Workers Order and the Human Rights Club. Mrs. Brown identified with her father's social activism and started participating in leftist activities during her high school years. She joined a picket line of garment workers in Chicago, and spent two summers at the leftist Commonwealth College in Mena, Arkansas. During these years, she also supported a group called the Spanish Loyalists. She attended both the University of Chicago and Northwestern University.

In 1947, Mrs. Brown became outraged when she heard about the deplorable condition of the Walker School, a Black school in the district, and the segregation policy used to justify the poor conditions. As a result of her outrage, Mrs. Brown became the grassroots face of the major movement in Merriam, Kansas to desegregate public education in the 1940s, and vehemently opposed the unequal treatment of Black students at the segregated Walker School, and in Topeka, Kansas. Initially, Mrs. Brown worked for equal education for the Black students, requesting improvements to the old dilapidated school building they attended while White South Park students attended a new state–of-the-art school building. However, Mrs. Brown would ultimately work for the actual desegregation of the entire school district, as she believes it to be the best way to achieve equality in education for Black students in 1954 with the decision of *Brown v. Board of Education*.

Development of Desegregation Policy

Mrs. Brown spearheaded the movement against the desegregation of public education in Merriam, Kansas through the local legal means available to the NAACP in the 1940s, starting with leading the negotiations with the local school board for the equal treatment of Black students at the Walker School to no avail. This movement evolved into a more organized national movement until the desegregation policy in education reached the U.S. Supreme Court for its final resolution in 1954 with *Brown v. Board of Education*.

One of the most significant roles that Mrs. Brown played in the local desegregation movement was raising public awareness about the condition of the dilapidated school for Black students in Topeka. Mrs. Brown's efforts and all the publicity that came with it made the region and the nation aware that there was a growing demand for a legal movement to dismantle segregation in public education in Kansas and across the nation. Therefore, her leadership paved the way for this unprecedented desegregation movement in public education in the 1950s.

Mrs. Brown's relentless local activism eventually united the Black community in Merriam. She organized their efforts and resources, and tapped the help of influential individuals in the community and nationally to help the community achieve their goal to desegregate local public schools.

Unsung Heroine

Mrs. Brown is an unsung heroine of the twentieth-century desegregation movement in the United States. She worked at the grassroots level of the desegregation of public education in Merriam, Kansas with minimal recognition. Although Mrs. Brown attended and spoke at board meetings, branch meetings, church services, convention gatherings, and forums, the recognition given to her was far from what the NAACP should have shown her considering her tireless contributions to the movement. The contemporary public narrative on desegregation policy has yet to place her in the same social justice limelight as other prominent activists of her time. Rather, the public narrative continues to shine the limelight only on the lawyers and the plaintiffs on record. Mrs. Brown received little recognition for all her efforts against segregation in public education compared to her Black male counterparts. The witnesses to her relentless activism were only those directly involved in her daily activism: the Black community in Topeka, staff and members of the local and national NAACP chapters and the members of the school board who antagonized her. The unpublicized communications she had with the community, lawyers and the NAACP have, until now, remained a silenced witness of the intelligent arguments she advanced for the local and national movement to desegregate public education. Most never saw her resolve in the midst of the frustrations she had in the many legal battles and delays with the *Webb* case.

The NAACP chose not to give Mrs. Brown the same recognition as Black male leaders such as Thurgood Marshall, the director of the NAACP legal department who would become the first African-American Supreme Court justice in 1967. Instead, the NAACP relegated Mrs. Brown's relentless activism to a place of invisibility in the contemporary narrative on desegregation in public education.

Critical Theory of Desegregation

In this historical narrative, this historian used a combination of Critical Race Theory and Black Feminist Theory to examine the roles of race, racism, sexism, and power in the desegregation of public education in Topeka, the capital city in Kansas, in the late 1940s and early 1950s. According to Critical Race Theory, the segregation policy of the South Park school board in the 1940s was a reflection of White supremacy and the subsequent subordination of the Black children at the segregated dilapidated Walker School. The segregation policy of the South Park school district served both the psychic and material purposes of the White community including the use of property taxes from the Black community in the operating budget of the South Park school district as voiced by one of the parents at the Walker School demanding equal treatment. Therefore, Topeka did not have any incentives in desegregating the school district until Mrs. Esther Brown and the NAACP with their equalization strategy led the movement to challenge the treatment of the Black students at the segregated Walker School. This type of systemic change proposed by Mrs. Brown and the NAACP required a critical pedagogy. Mrs. Brown challenged both the White and Black communities throughout the district and the state of Kansas to think critically about the impact of segregation on both the White and Black students in Topeka until she was able to wrought change in Topeka in the late 1940s with the help of the Kansas Supreme Court's decision in *Webb v. School District No. 90* (1949). Therefore, Critical Race Theory, as the theoretical framework for this historical narrative provided the guidance needed to begin to understand Mrs. Brown's role in the desegregation of public education in Topeka in the 1940s and 1950s.

The development of desegregation policy in education in the 1940s and 1950s through the uncompromised facilitation of key players such as Mrs. Esther Brown in the fight for equality and fairness enabled the nation to begin the process of dismantling racism in education. Critical Race Theory argues that racism and the issue of inequality are not fixed elements in society (Gall et al., 2003). As such, this theory indicates that a motivated person can change the social construct in a manner that creates a favorable condition for the entire population in a given society (Iggers, 1997). Therefore, this theory is the key in understanding the role that Mrs. Brown played in the development of desegregation policy in public education and the manner in which the desegregation policy changed public education in the United States.

However, to fully understand the significance of Mrs. Brown's fearless activism in the desegregation movement in Topeka and why she is an invisible heroine in the contemporary public narrative, we needed to understand the impact of not just the social construct of racism but also sexism in the 1940s. Mrs. Brown did not let the sexist behavior she experienced from her male counterparts in the movement to cause her to take her eyes off the goal of desegregating the South Park school district. Gender, race, and class biases are responsible for the invisibility of Mrs. Brown and others in the contemporary narrative on the desegregation of public education in the United States. The historical record shows that Thurgood Marshall did not want Mrs. Brown to be the face of the desegregation movement so he encouraged his male counterparts to get meaningfully involved in the arbitration and litigation of the South Park desegregation case.

The historical record does not indicate that Mrs. Brown identified herself as a feminist, but she clearly embodied feminist principles of empowerment. Mrs. Brown, a White Jewish woman with a strong heritage of social justice, became an ally in the second wave of the Black feminist movement in the Civil Rights Movement of the twentieth century as a result of her relentless activism in the desegregation movement in Topeka in the 1940s.

During Mrs. Brown's life and activism, Taylor (1998) states that there were "two waves" of Black feminist thought in the United States in the nineteenth and twentieth century. The first wave of feminism emerged out of the abolitionist movement (1830-1865) and culminated in the women's suffrage movement (1890-1920). During this 19th century period of women's struggle for freedom, Black women abolitionists developed a collective consciousness to dismantle the legal institution of slavery and sexual abuse. The second wave of feminism began with the Civil Rights Movement in the 1950s and culminated during the women's liberation movement of the 1960s. During this twentieth century period of struggle for equality with Title VII of the Civil Rights Act of 1964 and Voting Rights Act of 1965, Black feminist activists began to expose and confront male chauvinistic behavior of their counterparts in the civil rights movement and began to pressure the government to enforce Title VII, the legal protection of employment discrimination based on gender. Mrs. Esther Brown did not allow the sexist behavior she experienced from her male counterparts in Kansas and New York to deter her from the goal to desegregate public schools.

In conclusion, this historical narrative has been shaped by the Critical Race Theory's legal storytelling movement. This movement encourages people of color to write and recount experiences with racism and the legal system in such a way to challenge and change the master narrative. This historian has changed the contemporary public narrative on the desegregation of public education by researching and writing on the life and activism of Mrs. Esther Brown.

The Next Twenty Years

The successful outcome of *Webb v. School District No. 90* (1949) launched Mrs. Esther Brown into twenty years of fulltime community activism to desegregate public education and other public sectors locally and nationally, beginning with organizing the successful landmark civil rights case, *Brown v. Board of Education* (1954), to desegregate public education in the United States. In 1953, Mrs. Brown testified before the Kansas legislature to end discrimination in public employment. In 1957, Mrs. Brown helped to organize the first Panel of American Women with the mission to create dialogue and support among diverse groups of women and by 1970, Mrs. Brown had organized these panels in 63 cities with a membership of more than 14,000 women in the United States and Canada. In 1960s, the Jackson County Civil Rights Commission in Missouri appointed Mrs. Brown to their board. Unfortunately, her life and activism ended prematurely when she died from cancer on May 24, 1970 at the age of 53 (Katz & Tucker, Winter 1995/1996; Kaufman, 1989; Kluger, 2004; Speer, 1968; The JBHE Foundation, 2001).

Conclusion

Mrs. Esther Brown is a heroine in the desegregation movement in the United States. Although Mrs. Brown was relentless in her desegregation efforts in public education in the late 1940s and early 1950s, very few people know her name beyond the historians who have delved into the NAACP archives at the U.S. Library of Congress. Gender bias has created, in part, the invisibility of female leaders and activists like Mrs. Brown in social movement literature and feminist literature. The NAACP's gender bias was not just present in the desegregation movement in Topeka, but across the nation throughout the Civil Rights movement in the 1940s and 1950s (Barnett, 1993).

Mrs. Brown played a key role in establishing the Merriam branch of the NAACP in Kansas in the 1940s, organizing the Black community to support house and church schools to protest the segregation policy of their school district, and coordinating the desegregation of South Park School after engaging in an exhaustive writing campaign. This writing campaign serves as the historical record for this historical narrative, thanks to Mrs. Brown's intentional documentation of her relentless activism.

In the 1940s and 1950s, Mrs. Brown led by example (Delaurie, 2008, p. 8). She showed through her life example that if no one tells your story, it is your responsibility to tell your own story and do so in a way that will ensure that, seventy years from now, a historian will find your story of activism in the archives of your life and share your strength with the next generation.

ABOUT THE AUTHOR

Dr. Jessica Davis is the founder and president of the Faith and Public Policy Institute, Inc., a 501(c)(3) nonpartisan nonprofit organization, in Princeton, New Jersey. The mission of the Institute is to educate the faith community on domestic and foreign policy. Dr. Davis also serves as the senior pastor of St. Paul United Methodist Church in New Jersey. She is the first female pastor in the 130 year history of this historic Black congregation. Dr. Davis lectures in the areas of African American studies, American government and politics, comparative religion, constitutional law, ethics, international politics, and domestic and foreign policy.

Dr. Davis earned her Doctor of Philosophy from Southern Illinois University Carbondale, Doctor of Ministry from United Theological Seminary,

Juris Doctorate from Boston University School of Law, Master of Divinity from Boston University School of Theology, and Bachelor of Arts from Franklin and Marshall College.

To contact author, email her at
president@faithpolicyinstitute.org

BIBLIOGRAPHY

Appleby, J., Hunt, L., & Jacob, M. (1994). Telling the truth about history. New York, NY: W.W. Norton & Company, Inc.

Barnett, B. M. (1993). Invisible southern Black women leaders in the Civil Rights Movement: The triple constraints of gender, race, and class. Gender and Society, 7(2), 162-182.

Bell, D. (1980). Brown v. Board of Education and the interest-convergence dilemma. Harvard Law Review, 93(3), 518-33.

Bell, D. (2004). Brown v. Board of Education: Reliving and learning from our racial history. University of Pittsburgh Law Review, 66(21), 21-33.

Bloch, M. (1963). The historian's craft. New York, NY: Alfred A. Knopf, Inc.

Bombaro, C. (2012). Finding history: Research methods and resources for students and scholars. Toronto, UK: Scarecrow Press.

Bogdan, R. C., & Biklen, S. K. (2003). Qualitative research for education: An introduction to theories and methods (4th ed.). New York, NY: Pearson.

Borg, W., & Gall, M. D. (1983). Educational research: An introduction. New York, NY: Longman.

Brown, E. (1948a, August 4). Letter from Esther Brown [Letter to Edward R. Dudley]. National Association for the Advancement of Colored People Records, Library of Congress, Washington, DC.

Brown, E. (1948b, August 19). Letter from Esther Brown [Letter to Franklin H. Williams]. National Association for the Advancement of Colored People Records. Library of Congress, Washington, DC.

Brown, E. (1948c, August 30). Letter from Esther Brown [Letter to Franklin H. Williams]. National Association for the Advancement of Colored People Records. Library of Congress, Washington, DC.

Brown, E. (1948d, September). Letter from Esther Brown [Letter to Franklin H. Williams].

National Association for the Advancement of Colored People Records. Library of Congress, Washington, DC.

Brown, E. (1948e, November 18). Letter from Esther Brown [Letter to Franklin H. Williams]. National Association for the Advancement of Colored People Records. Library of Congress, Washington, DC.

Brown, E. (1948f, November 19). Letter from Esther Brown [Letter to Franklin H. Williams]. National Association for the Advancement of Colored People Records. Library of Congress, Washington, DC.

Brown, E. (1948g, November 28). Letter from Esther Brown [Letter to Franklin H. Williams]. National Association for the Advancement of Colored People Records. Library of Congress, Washington, DC.

Brown, E. (1948h, December). Letter from Esther Brown [Letter to Franklin H. Williams]. National Association for the Advancement of Colored People Records. Library of Congress, Washington, DC.

Brown, E. (1948i, December). Letter from Esther Brown [Letter to Franklin H. Williams]. National Association for the Advancement of Colored People Records. Library of Congress, Washington, DC.

Brown, E. (1948j, December 16). Letter from Esther Brown [Letter to Franklin H. Williams]. National Association for the Advancement of Colored People Records. Library of Congress, Washington, DC.

Brown, E. (1948k, December). Letter from Esther Brown [Letter to Franklin H. Williams]. National Association for the Advancement of Colored People Records. Library of Congress, Washington, DC.

Brown, E. (1948l, December 30). Letter from Esther Brown [Letter to Franklin H. Williams]. National Association for the Advancement of Colored People Records. Library of Congress, Washington, DC.

Brown, E. (1949a, January 13). Letter from Esther Brown [Letter to Franklin H. Williams]. National Association for the Advancement of

Colored People Records. Library of Congress, Washington, DC.

Brown, E. (1949b, January 21). Letter from Esther Brown [Letter to Franklin H. Williams]. National Association for the Advancement of Colored People Records. Library of Congress, Washington, DC.

Brown, E. (1949c, January 29). Letter from Esther Brown [Letter to Franklin H. Williams]. National Association for the Advancement of Colored People Records. Library of Congress, Washington, DC.

Brown, E. (1949d, February). Letter from Esther Brown [Letter to Franklin H. Williams]. National Association for the Advancement of Colored People Records. Library of Congress, Washington, DC.

Brown, E. (1949e, April 7). Letter from Esther Brown [Letter to Walter White]. National Association for the Advancement of Colored People Records. Library of Congress, Washington, DC.

Brown, E. (1949f, May 13). Letter from Esther Brown [Letter to Franklin H. Williams]. National

Association for the Advancement of Colored People Records. Library of Congress, Washington, DC.

Brown, E. (1949g, May). Letter from Esther Brown [Letter to Franklin H. Williams]. National Association for the Advancement of Colored People Records. Library of Congress, Washington, DC.

Brown, E. (1949h, June 5). Letter from Esther Brown [Letter to Franklin H. Williams]. National Association for the Advancement of Colored People Records. Library of Congress, Washington, DC.

Brown, E. (1949h, June). Letter from Esther Brown [Letter to Franklin H. Williams and Walter White]. National Association for the Advancement of Colored People Records. Library of Congress, Washington, DC.

Brown, E. (1949i, June 11). Telegram from Esther Brown [Telegram to Franklin H. Williams and Walter White]. National Association for the Advancement of Colored People Records. Library of Congress, Washington, DC.

Brown, E. (1949j, June 26). Letter from Esther Brown [Letter to Franklin H. Williams]. National Association for the Advancement of Colored People Records. Library of Congress, Washington, DC.

Brown, E. (1949k, July 5). Letter from Esther Brown [Letter to Franklin H. Williams]. National Association for the Advancement of Colored People Records. Library of Congress, Washington, DC.

Brown, E. (1949l, August 1). Letter from Esther Brown [Letter to Franklin H. Williams]. National Association for the Advancement of Colored People Records. Library of Congress, Washington, DC.

Brown, E. (1949m, August 16). Letter from Esther Brown [Letter to Franklin H. Williams]. National Association for the Advancement of Colored People Records. Library of Congress, Washington, DC.

Brown, E. (1949n, August 20). Letter from Esther Brown [Letter to Franklin H. Williams]. National Association for the Advancement of

Colored People Records. Library of Congress, Washington, DC.

Brown, E. (1949o, October). Letter from Esther Brown [Letter to Roy Wilkins]. National Association for the Advancement of Colored People Records. Library of Congress, Washington, DC.

Brownell, H. (1993). Brown v. Board of Education revisited. Journal of Supreme Court History, 18(1), 21-28.

Brown v. Board of Education, 347 U.S. 483 (1954).

Brown v. Board of Education (Brown II), 349 U.S. 294 (1955).

Brown v. Board of Education 50th Anniversary Commission, Pub. L. No. 107-41, 115 Stat. 226 (2001).

Burke, P. (Ed.). (1991). New perspectives on historical writing. University Park, PA: The Pennsylvania State University Press.

Byrne, D. N., Williams, J., & Thurgood Marshall Scholarship Fund. (2005). Brown v. Board of Education: Its impact on public education, 1954-2004. Brooklyn, NY: Word for Word Publishing Co.

Carr, E. H. (1961). What is history? New York, NY: Vintage Books.

Carter, R. L. (1949, January 25). Memorandum from Robert L. Carter [Memorandum to Franklin H. Williams]. National Association for the Advancement of Colored People Records. Library of Congress, Washington, DC.

Claire, S., & Lydia, B. (2011). Social context of education. Retrieved January 29, 2014, from http://www.oxfordbibliographies.com/view/d ocument/obo-9780199756810/obo-9780199756810-0039.xml.

Cound, J. J. (1998). A very new lawyer's first case: Brown v. Board of Education. Constitutional Commentary, 15, 57-64.

Crenshaw, K., Gotanda, N., Peller, G. & Thomas, K. (1995). Critical race theory: The key writings that formed the movement. New York, NY: The New Press.

Daniel, P. T. K. (2005). The not so strange path of desegregation in America's public schools. The Negro Educational Review, 56(1), 57-66.

Darder, A., Baltodano, M. & Torres, R. (Eds.). (2003). The critical pedagogy reader. New York, NY: RoutledgeFalmer.

Davis, A. P. (1948, December 27). Letter from A. Porter Davis [Letter to Franklin H. Williams]. National Association for the Advancement of Colored People Records. Library of Congress, Washington, DC.

Davis, J. J. (2016). The historical narrative on the role of Mrs. Esther Brown in the development of desegregation policy in public education (Doctoral dissertation). Southern Illinois University Carbondale.

Davis, D. M., Friend, J. & Caruthers, L. (2010). The fear of color. American Educational History Journal, 37(1/2), 331-345.

DeLaurie, M.B. (2008). Planting seeds of change: Ella Baker's radical rhetoric. Women's Studies in Communication, 31(1), 1-28.

Delgado, R., & Stefancic, J. (2000). Critical race theory: The cutting edge. Philadelphia, PA: Temple University Press.

Delgado, R., & Stefancic, J. (2001). Critical race theory: An introduction. New York, NY: New York University Press.

Denzin, N. K., & Lincoln, Y. S. (2000). Handbook of qualitative research. Newbury Park, CA: Sage.

Donahoo, S. (2006). Derailing desegregation: Legal effort to end racial segregation in higher education before and after Brown. Equity & Excellence in Education, 39(4), 291-301.

Dudley, E. R. (1948a, July 28). Letter from Edward R. Dudley [Letter to Charles P. Howard, Esq.]. National Association for the Advancement of Colored People Records. Library of Congress, Washington, DC.

Dudley, E. R. (1948b, July 28). Letter from Edward R. Dudley [Letter to William H. Towers, Esq.]. National Association for the Advancement of Colored People Records. Library of Congress, Washington, DC.

Dudley, E. R. (1948c, July 28). Letter from Edward R. Dudley [Letter to Alfonso Webb]. National Association for the Advancement of Colored

People Records. Library of Congress, Washington, DC.

Dudziak, M. L. (1988). Desegregation as a cold war imperative. Stanford Law Review, 41(1), 61-120.

Dudziak, M. L. (2000). Cold war civil rights: Race and the image of American democracy. Princeton, NJ: Princeton University Press.

Edwards, R., & Willie, C. (1998). Black power and white power in public education. Westport, CT: Praeger.

Elman, P., & Norman S. (1987). The solicitor general's office, Justice Frankfurter, and civil rights litigation, 1946-1960: An oral history. Harvard Law Review, 100(4), 817-52.

Expenditures in the Merriam Kansas school case. (1948, January 10). National Association for the Advancement of Colored People Records. Library of Congress, Washington, DC.

Fairclough, N. (2010). Critical discourse analysis: The critical study of language (2 ed.). New York, NY: Routledge.

Fasset, J. D. (1986). Mr. Justice Reed and Brown v. The Board of Education. Yearbook of the Supreme Court Historical Society, 48-63.

Financial statement on the South Park, Merriam, Kansas. (1949, May 21). National Association for the Advancement of Colored People Records. Library of Congress, Washington, DC.

Flower, F.C. (2004). Policy studies for educational leaders. Upper Saddle River, NJ: Pearson Education, Inc.

Freire, P. (1993). Pedagogy of the oppressed. New York, NY: The Continuum International Publishing Group Inc.

Freire, P. (1998). Pedagogy of freedom. New York, NY: Rowman & Littlefield Publishers, Inc.

Gall, S. P., Gall, M. O. & Borg, W. R. (1999). Applying educational research: A practical guide (4th ed.). New York, NY: Longman.

Gall, M. D., Gall, J. P., & Borg, W. R. (2003). Educational research an introduction (7th ed.). Boston, MA: Allyn.

Garner, B.A. (1995). A dictionary of modern legal usage. Oxford, NY: Oxford University Press.

Gilderhus, M.T. (2003). History and historians: A historiographical introduction. Upper Saddle River, NJ: Pearson Education, Inc.

Graham v. The Board of Education of the City of Topeka, 153 Kan. 843 (1941).

Green, A. & Troup, K. (1999). The houses of history: A critical reader in twentieth-century history and theory. New York, NY: New York University Press.

Hinchey, P.H. (2004). Becoming a critical educator: Defining a classroom Identity, designing a critical pedagogy. New York, NY: Peter Lang.

Holmes, L.S. (1949, February 17). Letter from Laurence S. Holmes [Letter to Franklin H. Williams]. National Association for the Advancement of Colored People Records. Library of Congress, Washington, DC.

Howard, C. (1948, August 19). Memorandum from Charles Howard [Memorandum to Thurgood Marshall]. National Association for the Advancement of Colored People Records. Library of Congress, Washington, DC.

Howard, C. (1949, April 14). Letter from Charles Howard [Letter to Walter White]. National Association for the Advancement of Colored People Records. Library of Congress, Washington, DC.

Howell, M. & Prevenier, W. (2001). From reliable sources: An introduction to historical methods. New York, NY: Cornell University Press.

Hunter, R. C. (2011). Public school desegregation and education facilities. School Business Affairs, 77, 24-26.

Iggers, G.G. (1997). Historiography in the twentieth century: From scientific objectivity to the postmodern challenge. Middletown, CT: Wesleyan University Press.

Ira, S. (1999). Culture wars: School and society in the conservative restoration 1969-1984. Chicago: University of Chicago Press.

Jamar, S. D. (2004). Retrieved May 25, 2008, from http://www.brownat50.org/brownBios/BioCharlesHHouston.html.

Jasper, M.C. (2009). Dictionary of selected legal terms. Oxford, NY: Oxford University Press.

Johnson, A. (1997). Privilege, power, and difference. New York, NY: McGraw-Hill.

Johnson, C. R. (1948a, December 23). Telegram from Carl R. Johnson [Telegram to Franklin H. Williams]. National Association for the Advancement of Colored People Records. Library of Congress, Washington, DC.

Johnson, C. R. (1949a, January 19). Letter from Carl R. Johnson [Letter to Franklin H. Williams]. National Association for the Advancement of Colored People Records. Library of Congress, Washington, DC.

Johnson, C. R. (1949b, January 27). Letter from Carl R. Johnson [Letter to Elisha Scott]. National Association for the Advancement of Colored People Records. Library of Congress, Washington, DC.

Johnson, C. R. (1949c, March 5). Letter from Carl R. Johnson [Letter to Elisha Scott]. National Association for the Advancement of Colored People Records. Library of Congress, Washington, DC.

Kaufman, J. (1989). Broken alliance: The turbulent times between Blacks and Jews in America. New York, NY: New American Library.

Katz, S. & Tucker, S. B. (Winter 1995/1996). A pioneer in Civil Rights: Esther Brown and the South Park desegregation case of 1948. Kansas History, 18, 234-247.

Klarman, M. J. (1994). Brown, racial change, and the civil rights movement. Virginia Law Review, 80(1), 7-150.

Klarman, M. J. (2004). From Jim Crow to civil rights: The Supreme Court and racial equality. New York, NY: Oxford University Press.

Klarman, M. J. (2007). Brown v. Board of Education and the civil rights movement. New York, NY: Oxford University Press.

Kluger, R. (2004). Simple justice: The history of Brown v. Board of Education and Black America's struggle for equality. New York, NY: Alfred A. Knopf.

Kozol, J. (2005). Still separate, still unequal: America's educational apartheid. Harper's Magazine, 311, 1864.

Kumar, A. (2014). Social research methods. New Delhi: McGraw Hill Education.

Kumashiro, K. (2004). Against common sense: Teaching and learning toward social justice. New York, NY: RoutledgeFalmer.

Lawrence, S. (1949, June 24). Letter from Sidney Lawrence [Letter to Esther Brown]. National Association for the Advancement of Colored People Records. Library of Congress, Washington, DC.

Lawson, S. F., & Charles, P. (2006). Debating the civil rights movement, 1945-1968. New York, NY: Rowman & Littlefield Publishers, Inc.

Little, K. (2009). You must be from the North: Southern white women in the Memphis Civil Rights Movement. Jackson, MS: University of Mississippi Press.

Makes appeal for worthy cause (1948, November 26). The Call, National Association for the Advancement of Colored People Records. Library of Congress, Washington, DC.

Manhattan folk hear talk on South Park case. (1949, May 20). The Call. National Association for the

Advancement of Colored People Records. Library of Congress, Washington, DC.

Manz, W. H. (2004). Brown v. Board of Education. Law Library Journal, 96(2), 246-266.

Marius, R. & Page, M.E. (2007). A short guide to writing about history. New York, NY: Pearson Education, Inc.

Marshall, T. (1948a, August 23). Memorandum from Thurgood Marshall [Memorandum to Franklin H. Williams]. National Association for the Advancement of Colored People Records. Library of Congress, Washington, DC.

Marshall, T. (1948b, November 30). Telegram from Thurgood Marshall [Telegram to Elisha Scott]. National Association for the Advancement of Colored People Records. Library of Congress, Washington, DC.

Marshall, T. (1949a, January 27). Letter from Thurgood Marshall [Letter to Elisha Scott]. National Association for the Advancement of Colored People Records. Library of Congress, Washington, DC.

Maruca, M. (2004). Brown v. Board of Education historical handbook. Western National Park Association.

Mayer, M. (1986). With much deliberation and some speed: Eisenhower and the Brown decision. Journal of Southern History, 52(1), 43-76.

McConnell, M. (1995). Originalism and the desegregation decisions. Virginia Law Review, 81(4), 947-1140.

McConnell, M. (1996). The originalist case for Brown v. Board of Education. Harvard Journal of Law and Public Policy, 19, 457-464.

McMiller, D. L. (2000). Public Opinion and School Desegregation in Hartford, Connecticut. Equity & Excellence in Education, 33(2), 68-80.

McNeil, G. R. (1983). Groundwork: Charles Hamilton Houston and the struggle for civil rights. Philadelphia, PA: University of Pennsylvania.

Meier, A. (1963). Negro movements and organizations. Journal of Negro Education, 32(4), 437-450.

Monhollon, R. & Oertel, K. T. (2004). From Brown to Brown. Kansas History, 27(1/2), 116-135.

Motley, C. B. (1992). The historical setting of Brown and its impact on the Supreme Court's decision. Fordham Law Review, 61(1), 9-17.

NAACP (2008). NAACP legal history. Retrieved May 25, 2008, from http://www.brownat50.org/brownBios/BioCh arlesHHouston.html.

Novick, P. (1988). That noble dream: The "objectivity question" and the American historical profession. New York, NY: Cambridge University Press.

Paige, R. (2002). Remarks by U.S. Secretary of Education Rod Paige to the Brown v. Board of Education 50th anniversary commission, Howard University School of Law (speech, November 13, 2002).

Perna, L., Gerald, D., Baum, E., & Milem, J. (2007). The status of equity for black faculty and administrators in public higher education in the south. Research in Higher Education, 48, 193-228.

Petition fails to halt Kansas School Jim Crow (1948, December 16). National Association for the

Advancement of Colored People Records. Library of Congress, Washington, DC.

Philip, T. M. (2012). Desegregation, the attack on public education, and the inadvertent critiques of social justice educators: Implications for teacher education. Teacher Education Quarterly, 39(2), 29-41.

Plessy v. Ferguson, 163 U.S. 537 (1896).

Press release (1948, December 15). National Association for the Advancement of Colored People Records. Library of Congress, Washington, DC.

Roberts, C. M. (2010). The dissertation journey: A practical and comprehensive guide to planning, writing, and defending your dissertation (2 ed.). New York: SAGE Publications.

Rosenblum, T. (2008). The segregation of Topeka's public school system, 1879-1951. National Park Service.

Rossell, C. H., Armor, D. J., & Walberg, H. J. (2002). School desegregation in the 21st century. Connecticut: Praeger.

Schaack, B. V. (2004). With all deliberate speed: Civil human rights litigation as a tool for social change. Vanderbilt Law Review, 57, 2305-2348.

Scott, E. (1948a, August 7). Letter from Elisha Scott [Letter to Legal Department, NAACP]. National Association for the Advancement of Colored People Records. Library of Congress, Washington, DC.

Scott, E. (1948b, August 16). Letter from Elisha Scott [Letter to Esther E. Brown]. National Association for the Advancement of Colored People Records. Library of Congress, Washington, DC.

Scott, E. (1948c, November 26). Letter from Elisha Scott [Letter to Esther E. Brown]. National Association for the Advancement of Colored People Records. Library of Congress, Washington, DC.

Scott, E. (1949a, January 22). Letter from Elisha Scott [Letter to Thurgood Marshall]. National Association for the Advancement of Colored People Records. Library of Congress, Washington, DC.

Scott, E. (1949b, February 1). Letter from Elisha Scott [Letter to Thurgood Marshall]. National Association for the Advancement of Colored People Records. Library of Congress, Washington, DC.

Scott, E. (1949c, February 23). Letter from Elisha Scott [Letter to Franklin H. Williams]. National Association for the Advancement of Colored People Records. Library of Congress, Washington, DC.

Scott, E. (1949d, February 25). Telegram from Elisha Scott [Telegram to Franklin H. Williams]. National Association for the Advancement of Colored People Records. Library of Congress, Washington, DC.

Scott, E. (1949e, March 21). Letter from Elisha Scott [Letter to Franklin H. Williams]. National Association for the Advancement of Colored People Records. Library of Congress, Washington, DC.

Scott, E. (1949f, April 21). Letter from Elisha Scott [Letter to Thurgood Marshall]. National Association for the Advancement of Colored

People Records. Library of Congress, Washington, DC.

Skocpol, T. (Ed.). (1984). Vision and method in historical sociology. New York, NY: Cambridge University Press.

Speer, H. W. (1968). The case of the century: A historical and social perspective on Brown v. Board of Education of Topeka. Kansas City, MO: University of Missouri Press.

Storey, W. K. (2004). Writing history: A guide for students. New York, NY: Oxford University Press.

Sum, P. E., Light, S. A., & King, R. F. (2004). Race, reform, and desegregation in Mississippi higher education: Historically Black institutions after United States v. Fordice. Law & Social Inquiry, 29(2), 403-435.

Taylor, W.E. (1948, December 13). Letter from Wesley E. Taylor [Letter to Esther E. Brown]. National Association for the Advancement of Colored People Records. Library of Congress, Washington, DC.

The JBHE Foundation (2001). Remembering Esther Brown: She was responsible for the first break in segregated education. The Journal of Blacks in Higher Education, 34, 76.

Tyack, D. & Lowe, R. (1986). The constitutional moment: Reconstruction and black education in the south. American Journal of Education, 94(2), 236-256.

Waugh, D. (2012). The issue is the control of public schools: The politics of desegregation in Prince Edward County, Virginia. Southern Cultures, 18, 76-94.

Webb v. School District No. 90, 167 Kan. 395 (1949).

Wetmore, Z. (1949, January 20). Letter from the Law Offices of Wetmore and Ashford [Letter to Esther E. Brown]. National Association for the Advancement of Colored People Records. Library of Congress, Washington, DC.

Williams, F. H. (1948a, August 6). Letter from Franklin H. Williams [Letter to Esther E. Brown]. National Association for the Advancement of Colored People Records. Library of Congress, Washington, DC.

Williams, F. H. (1948b, August 11). Memorandum from Franklin H. Williams [Memorandum to Thurgood Marshall]. National Association for the Advancement of Colored People Records. Library of Congress, Washington, DC.

Williams, F. H. (1948c, August 17). Letter from Franklin H. Williams [Letter to Esther E. Brown]. National Association for the Advancement of Colored People Records. Library of Congress, Washington, DC.

Williams, F. H. (1948d, August 26). Memorandum from Franklin H. Williams [Memorandum to Thurgood Marshall]. National Association for the Advancement of Colored People Records. Library of Congress, Washington, DC.

Williams, F. H. (1948e, October 6). Memorandum from Franklin H. Williams [Memorandum to Thurgood Marshall]. National Association for the Advancement of Colored People Records. Library of Congress, Washington, DC.

Williams, F. H. (1948f, November 30). Letter from Franklin H. Williams [Letter to Esther E. Brown]. National Association for the

Advancement of Colored People Records. Library of Congress, Washington, DC.

Williams, F. H. (1948g, December 1). Memorandum from Franklin H. Williams [Memorandum to Henry Lee Moon]. National Association for the Advancement of Colored People Records. Library of Congress, Washington, DC.

Williams, F. H. (1948h, December 2). Telegram from Franklin H. Williams [Telegram to Esther E. Brown]. National Association for the Advancement of Colored People Records. Library of Congress, Washington, DC.

Williams, F. H. (1948i, December 15). Letter from Franklin H. Williams [Letter to Esther E. Brown]. National Association for the Advancement of Colored People Records. Library of Congress, Washington, DC.

Williams, F. H. (1948j, December 21). Letter from Franklin H. Williams [Letter to Carl R. Brown]. National Association for the Advancement of Colored People Records. Library of Congress, Washington, DC.

Williams, F. H. (1948k, December 22). Letter from Franklin H. Williams [Letter to E.A. Freeman]. National Association for the Advancement of Colored People Records. Library of Congress, Washington, DC.

Williams, F. H. (1948l, December 22). Letter from Franklin H. Williams [Letter to Esther E. Brown]. National Association for the Advancement of Colored People Records. Library of Congress, Washington, DC.

Williams, F. H. (1949a, January 5). Letter from Franklin H. Williams [Letter to Esther E. Brown]. National Association for the Advancement of Colored People Records. Library of Congress, Washington, DC.

Williams, F. H. (1949b, January 7). Letter from Franklin H. Williams [Letter to Charles Bettis]. National Association for the Advancement of Colored People Records. Library of Congress, Washington, DC.

Williams, F. H. (1949c, January 20). Letter from Franklin H. Williams [Letter to Esther E. Brown]. National Association for the

Advancement of Colored People Records. Library of Congress, Washington, DC.

Williams, F. H. (1949d, January 28). Letter from Franklin H. Williams [Letter to Carl R. Johnson]. National Association for the Advancement of Colored People Records. Library of Congress, Washington, DC.

Williams, F. H. (1949e, January 28). Letter from Franklin H. Williams [Letter to Elisha Scott]. National Association for the Advancement of Colored People Records. Library of Congress, Washington, DC.

Williams, F. H. (1949f, February 14). Letter from Franklin H. Williams [Letter to Elisha Scott]. National Association for the Advancement of Colored People Records. Library of Congress, Washington, DC.

Williams, F. H. (1949g, February 23). Letter from Franklin H. Williams [Letter to Laurence S. Holmes]. National Association for the Advancement of Colored People Records. Library of Congress, Washington, DC.

Williams, F. H. (1949h, February 25). Letter from Franklin H. Williams [Letter to Esther E. Brown]. National Association for the Advancement of Colored People Records. Library of Congress, Washington, DC.

Williams, F. H. (1949i, March 4). Letter from Franklin H. Williams [Letter to Esther E. Brown]. National Association for the Advancement of Colored People Records. Library of Congress, Washington, DC.

Williams, F. H. (1949j, March 21). Letter from Franklin H. Williams [Letter to Esther E. Brown]. National Association for the Advancement of Colored People Records. Library of Congress, Washington, DC.

Williams, F. H. (1949k, March 28). Letter from Franklin H. Williams [Letter to Esther E. Brown]. National Association for the Advancement of Colored People Records, Library of Congress, Washington, DC.

Williams, F. H. (1949l, April). Memorandum from Franklin H. Williams [Memorandum to Publicity Department]. National Association for the Advancement of Colored People Records. Library of Congress, Washington, DC.

Williams, F. H. (1949m, April 14). Letter from Franklin H. Williams [Letter to Esther E. Brown]. National Association for the Advancement of Colored People Records. Library of Congress, Washington, DC.

Williams, F. H. (1949n, May 3). Letter from Franklin H. Williams [Letter to Esther E. Brown]. National Association for the Advancement of Colored People Records. Library of Congress, Washington, DC.

Williams, F. H. (1949o, June 17). Letter from Franklin H. Williams [Letter to Esther E. Brown]. National Association for the Advancement of Colored People Records. Library of Congress, Washington, DC.

Williams, F. H. (1949p, June 28). Memorandum from Franklin H. Williams [Memorandum to Gloster B. Current]. National Association for the Advancement of Colored People Records. Library of Congress, Washington, DC.

Williams, F. H. (1949q, July 29). Letter from Franklin H. Williams [Letter to Esther E. Brown]. National Association for the Advancement of Colored People Records. Library of Congress, Washington, DC.

Willie, C.V. (2005). The contribution of Brown v. Board of Education to law and democratic development. Syracuse Journal of Internal Law, 33(1), 115-130.

Willie, C. V., & Willie, S. S. (2005). Black, White, and Brown: The transformation of public education in America. Teachers College Record, 107, 475-495.

Yeazell, S. C. (2004). Brown, the civil rights movement and the silent litigation revolution. Vanderbilt Law Review, 57, 1975-2003

INDEX

A

abandon 34, 41
abolition 33
abolitionist 91
abolitionists 92
abuse 73, 92
academic 73, 80
accusations 67
accused 47, 73
activism 2, 4, 5, 7, 9, 10, 12, 13, 28, 33, 64, 74, 80, 83, 84, 86, 87, 88, 90, 91, 93, 95
activist 21, 83
activists 30, 87, 92, 94
administration 13
admit 13, 25
admitted 22, 63, 65
advice 25
advisable 69
advise 68
advised 17, 49
advocacy 54
advocate 36
advocating 22
affairs 8, 36
affiliation 30
affirmative 53
african 2, 3
african-american 88
agencies 61
agency 13
aggravate 43

aggressively 9
agitation 35
agitator 74
agree 27, 43, 57, 67, 70
agreed 37, 42, 44, 47, 51, 56, 57, 65, 76, 77, 78
agreeing 76
agreement 52
alfonso 17, 22
alive 20
alleged 30
allies 4, 77
allocate 70
allotted 75, 78
allow 20, 22, 68, 92
allowed 9
all-white 9, 10, 62, 80
ally 82, 91
america 4, 82
american 2, 3, 16, 61, 66, 93
american-born 6, 83
amicus 60, 61
annals 2
anniversary 1
antagonism 66
antagonized 87
apathy 39, 74
appeal 38, 49
appealed 33
appointed 93
appointment 27
appreciated 41
appreciating 50
apprehensive 60
apprised 26, 50

approval 16, 18, 61
approve 54
approved 7, 57, 60
april 22, 60, 62, 64
arbitrarily 26, 63
arbitrariness 24
arbitration 91
archives 94, 95
argue 26, 30
argued 17, 19, 47, 56, 62, 63
argues 90
arguing 45
argument 26, 43, 56, 57, 60
arguments 31, 33, 87
arkansas 7, 13, 84
army 13
article 55, 58
articles 75
associates 24
association 71, 75, 76
attack 21
attacks 35
attempt 13
attempted 21
attempts 70
attendance 75
attorney 18, 25, 27, 31, 36, 39, 40, 43, 44, 63
attorneys 49, 63
august 27, 75
authorities 17
authorized 57, 60
authorizing 38
aware 7, 16, 39, 59, 86
awareness 2, 27, 40, 55, 85

B

borrowing 37

boycott 2, 9, 32, 33, 38

branch 11, 18, 27, 29, 30, 31, 34, 35, 36, 37, 38, 39, 42, 43, 44, 45, 46, 48, 49, 50, 51, 53, 54, 57, 58, 59, 64, 68, 76, 77, 78, 80, 86, 94

branches 35, 36, 39, 51, 53

brawl 45

bribing 53

brief 6, 56, 60, 69

briefed 50

briefs 61

brown 1, 2, 3, 4, 5, 6, 7, 8, 9, 10, 12, 13, 16, 17, 18, 19, 20, 21, 22, 23, 24, 25, 26, 27, 28, 29, 30, 31, 32, 33, 34, 35, 36, 37, 38, 39, 40, 41, 42, 43, 44, 45, 46, 47, 48, 49, 50, 51, 52, 53, 54, 55, 56, 57, 58, 59, 60, 61, 62, 64, 65, 66, 67, 68, 69, 70, 71, 72, 73, 74, 75, 76, 77, 78, 79, 80, 81, 82, 83, 84, 85, 86, 87, 89, 90, 91, 92, 93, 94, 95

brunette 6

build 7, 16, 19, 78

building 15, 16, 17, 18, 85

built 15

bureau 9, 61, 68

burney 47, 48

burning 9, 22

businesswoman 8

byrne 3

C

cafeteria 8

called 7, 16, 33, 37, 54, 76, 78, 84

calls 22, 35, 52

campbell 19

cancel 1

cancer 6, 12, 93

capabilities 77

capital 88

captain 10

car 46

carl 49

carrie 47, 48

carried 33, 41

carter 57, 77

case 1, 10, 11, 14, 20, 25, 26, 27, 28, 29, 30, 32, 33,
34, 35, 36, 37, 38, 39, 40, 41, 42, 43, 44, 45, 46, 47,
48, 49, 50, 51, 52, 55, 56, 57, 58, 60, 61, 62, 63, 64,
65, 66, 67, 68, 69, 74, 75, 76, 80, 81, 87, 91, 93

cases 36

casey 63

casualties 55

catered 77

cause 38, 64, 77, 90

caused 32, 48

century 1, 15, 91, 92

ceremony 66

chair 20, 21

chairman 20

chairs 52

challenge 6, 8, 10, 54, 89, 92

challenged 2, 6, 83, 89

challenges 39, 42, 49

challenging 16, 41, 47, 48, 74, 80

change 2, 5, 9, 89, 90, 92

chapter 1, 5, 9, 12, 15, 17, 18, 24, 27, 28, 33, 38, 39,
49, 63, 80, 82

chapters 29, 39, 87

chauvinistic 92

chicago 7, 12, 84
chief 62, 74, 76
child 1
childhood 7, 13
children 2, 7, 8, 9, 15, 16, 17, 19, 22, 24, 25, 26, 31,
34, 36, 40, 42, 44, 49, 51, 53, 55, 59, 63, 65, 66, 69,
71, 72, 73, 78, 88
choice 59
chord 33
church 44, 45, 59, 86, 94
churches 17, 74
circulate 69
circulated 71, 78
circumstances 51
circumvent 65, 70
cities 56, 93
city 6, 7, 12, 13, 18, 26, 28, 29, 35, 36, 37, 38, 45, 46,
49, 50, 51, 54, 61, 66, 67, 68, 83, 88
civil 1, 2, 5, 7, 11, 27, 29, 66, 81, 91, 92, 93, 94
claiming 38
claire 3
class 90
classes 34, 43, 51
classroom 75
classrooms 19
clear 83
clearly 91
clerk 71
clock 25
close 20, 35, 39
closed 72
club 6, 12, 66, 84
coal 52, 64
co-authored 61

defected 53
defectors 53
defend 71
defendants 26, 31
defendant's 60
defended 29
defense 11, 81
degree 18
delaurie 95
delay 26, 31, 40, 41, 44, 52, 55, 56, 57, 71
delayed 25, 43, 52, 56, 62
delaying 57
delays 27, 39, 40, 52, 60, 87
delegates 33
delegation 76
deliberate 39, 52
demand 18, 22, 24, 86
demanded 22
demanding 70, 89
demands 18, 23, 25
demonstrates 50
denial 44
denied 21, 43
deny 1
denying 19
department 36, 41, 42, 82, 88
depended 4
deplorable 84
desegregate 10, 48, 53, 70, 74, 80, 83, 84, 86, 87, 92, 93
desegregated 10
desegregating 3, 89, 90
desegregation 1, 2, 3, 4, 5, 6, 16, 21, 23, 24, 26, 28, 29, 30, 31, 32, 33, 34, 35, 36, 38, 39, 40, 42, 45, 47,

duty 58

E

editorial 61
educated 1
educating 40
education 1, 2, 3, 4, 5, 6, 10, 15, 19, 22, 48, 49, 50, 52, 73, 74, 81, 82, 83, 84, 85, 86, 87, 88, 89, 90, 91, 93, 94
educational 21, 22, 31, 68
edward 29
edwin 19
eight 19, 59
elect 60
elected 65
election 30, 54
elisha 27, 73
embargo 20
emergency 40, 43, 44
employed 69
empowerment 91
encourage 78
encouraged 34, 58, 83, 91
endure 32
enroll 34, 36, 77
enrolled 13, 78
epistolary 41
equalization 32, 83, 89
equalize 21
establish 18, 23
established 15
establishing 94
establishment 72

estate 65

esther 2, 4, 5, 6, 7, 10, 12, 13, 16, 22, 82, 83, 89, 92, 93, 94

ethical 12

expenditures 52

expenses 38, 52, 64, 67

exposing 72

extensive 37, 67

eyes 16, 90

F

facilitation 89

facility 2, 15, 22, 26, 45, 56, 67, 70

fact 24, 54, 58

failure 29

fairness 89

fame 31, 48

families 10, 15, 29, 31, 40, 42, 61, 75

family 3, 13, 22, 82

father 6, 12, 17, 84

feared 58, 61, 65

fearless 82, 90

february 18, 58, 60

federal 9

federated 66

federation 61, 68

fee 25, 26, 37, 42, 76

female 16, 94

feminism 91, 92

feminist 82, 88, 91, 92, 94

fifty 5

fight 2, 22, 29, 30, 34, 40, 46, 53, 54, 65, 67, 70, 89

fighting 10, 13, 66

I

J

jackson 93
january 18, 41, 52, 55, 56
jbhe 5, 7, 8, 9, 10, 11, 13, 14, 16, 18, 19, 20, 21, 22, 23, 24, 81, 94
jewish 2, 6, 12, 61, 68, 82, 83, 91
jim 8, 30, 33, 51, 52, 77
johnson 15, 28, 35, 49, 50, 51, 52, 54, 55, 56, 57, 61, 68, 76, 77
joined 7, 12, 34, 84
joining 13
jones 63
journal 6
judge 43, 61
judgment 43
judicial 69
july 28, 71
juncture 73
june 67, 68
jurisdiction 15, 36, 43, 70
justice 40, 62, 76, 87, 88, 91
justify 8, 84

K

kansas 2, 4, 5, 6, 7, 9, 10, 12, 13, 18, 25, 26, 28, 29, 30, 33, 35, 36, 37, 38, 39, 45, 46, 47, 49, 50, 51, 52, 54, 55, 56, 57, 58, 60, 61, 62, 63, 64, 66, 67, 68, 69, 70, 72, 80, 82, 83, 84, 85, 86, 88, 89, 92, 93, 94
katz 5, 7, 8, 9, 10, 11, 13, 14, 16, 18, 19, 20, 21, 22, 23, 24, 34, 81, 94
kaufman 5, 7, 8, 9, 10, 11, 13, 14, 16, 18, 19, 20, 21, 22, 23, 24, 81, 94

manz 1

marriage 3, 9, 12, 29, 41, 42, 56, 57, 82, 83, 88, 91

married 7, 13

maslow 61

master 92

material 88

meeting 17, 18, 19, 22, 24, 31, 37, 45, 46, 47, 49, 54, 60, 66, 69, 78

meetings 39, 72, 86

meier 4

members 9, 18, 29, 32, 38, 39, 42, 46, 47, 54, 58, 60, 66, 73, 77, 78, 87

membership 48, 93

memberships 67

mena 7, 13, 84

methodist 21

mid-august 76

militant 29

military 9

millionaire 16

minister 10, 21, 80

miscarriage 10

missouri 6, 7, 12, 13, 49, 50, 54, 66, 67, 68, 83, 93

mobilized 2

moment 74

monetary 27, 35, 54, 58

money 2, 9, 17, 27, 37, 38, 39, 40, 42, 45, 46, 51, 53, 54, 55, 56, 58, 59, 61, 64, 65, 67, 73, 74, 75, 78

moral 50, 58

morale 58

morals 73

mother 6, 12, 55, 83, 84

motion 27, 31, 54, 58, 60, 70, 75, 76, 77

motions 57

movement 21, 29, 31, 38, 50, 55, 66, 70, 74, 75, 82, 83, 84, 85, 86, 87, 89, 90, 91, 92, 94

mrs 2, 3, 4, 5, 6, 7, 8, 9, 10, 11, 12, 16, 17, 18, 19, 20, 21, 22, 23, 24, 25, 26, 27, 28, 29, 30, 31, 32, 33, 34, 35, 36, 37, 38, 39, 40, 41, 42, 43, 44, 45, 46, 47, 48, 49, 50, 51, 52, 53, 54, 55, 56, 57, 58, 59, 60, 61, 62, 64, 65, 66, 67, 68, 69, 70, 71, 72, 73, 74, 75, 76, 77, 78, 79, 80, 81, 82, 83, 84, 85, 86, 87, 88, 89, 90, 91, 92, 93, 94, 95

N

naacp 5, 9, 10, 11, 17, 18, 22, 25, 26, 27, 28, 29, 30, 31, 32, 33, 34, 35, 36, 37, 38, 39, 41, 42, 43, 44, 45, 46, 47, 48, 49, 51, 52, 53, 55, 57, 58, 59, 63, 64, 65, 67, 68, 70, 72, 74, 75, 77, 78, 80, 81, 82, 83, 85, 86, 87, 88, 89, 94

naacp-supported 66

name-calling 35

narrative 4, 6, 82, 87, 88, 89, 90, 91, 92, 93, 95

narratives 5

nation 3, 4, 11, 61, 81, 86, 90, 94

national 5, 22, 26, 28, 29, 30, 35, 39, 41, 44, 45, 46, 49, 50, 51, 52, 53, 54, 55, 59, 63, 68, 70, 75, 77, 85, 87

nationally 86, 93

nationwide 42

negotiations 85

negro 15, 47, 66

neighborhood 7, 12, 83

newton 66

nigger 35

noncompliance 70

northeast 77

northwestern 7, 84
nose 36

O

obscenities 20
offer 19
offered 17, 26, 40, 42
offering 53
offers 19
office 46, 48, 49, 50, 51, 54, 55, 59, 70
officers 25, 29, 34, 39
ohio 68
one-room 15
one-woman 29
opponents 48
organizations 6, 12, 74, 84
osawatomie 33
outcome 80, 93
outcomes 25
outhouse 8, 17
outrage 84
owners 65

P

paige 1
park 2, 3, 7, 9, 14, 15, 16, 20, 21, 22, 25, 28, 29, 31,
33, 34, 36, 43, 44, 49, 50, 59, 62, 63, 65, 66, 67, 68,
69, 70, 72, 73, 74, 75, 76, 77, 78, 80, 85, 88, 90, 91,
95
parkers 36
parties 56
party 30, 50

pass 24, 46, 63
passed 12, 24, 46, 65
passion 13, 83
patrons 78
paul 7, 13
pay 5, 25, 27, 37, 39, 50, 51, 75, 77
payment 19, 45, 64
peace 35
pedagogy 89
pending 36, 43
people 20, 34, 35, 38, 39, 40, 44, 46, 48, 61, 67, 69, 71, 72, 73, 74, 75, 76, 92, 94
petition 43, 69, 70, 71, 75, 78
petitioners 43, 56
petitions 72, 75, 78
pharmacist 20
phone 19, 22, 52
photographer 55
photographs 55, 58, 61
photos 55, 61
picket 7, 12, 13, 84
picture 29, 49
pictures 5, 42, 55, 58
pillar 48
pioneers 4, 5
plaintiff 10, 80
plaintiffs 2, 10, 25, 36, 62, 80, 87
pleading 9
pleadings 56
pledged 54
plumbing 8
pocket 28, 52
policies 7, 8, 9

policy 1, 2, 3, 4, 5, 6, 8, 16, 22, 84, 85, 87, 88, 89, 90, 94

political 13, 30, 50

pools 68

poor 2, 60, 84

poorly 17

population 90

porter 18

postponed 18, 31, 57, 60

postponement 40

power 72, 88

practice 2, 3

practiced 26

praise 57

praised 63

premature 47

prematurely 93

presided 45, 66

president 18, 38, 45, 46, 47, 49, 54, 68

presidential 30

press 33, 42, 43

pressed 3

prices 65

primary 5, 59

proceedings 37, 74

progressive 13, 30

propaganda 53

protection 4, 92

psychic 88

public 1, 2, 3, 4, 5, 6, 10, 11, 13, 21, 22, 36, 42, 48, 49, 50, 80, 81, 82, 83, 84, 85, 86, 87, 88, 89, 90, 91, 92, 93, 94

publications 61

publicity 31, 33, 34, 40, 42, 58, 86

publicize 61, 67
publicized 54
publish 55
published 5
pupils 53, 59, 60
purpose 4, 48
purposes 67, 88

Q

qualified 19
question 40, 47
questioned 41

R

race 26, 68, 88, 89, 90, 92
racial 2, 6, 11, 15, 21, 60, 81, 83
racially 10, 26, 80
racism 88, 90, 92
racist 20, 21
raffle 46
railroad 10, 80
rainy 31
rally 36
rat 8
read 46, 58
reading 46, 56, 76
reallocation 35
receipt 50
refurbishing 18
region 86
regional 5
register 62, 78

S

sacrifice 73
sacrificed 82
sacrifices 66, 67, 78
salaries 37, 51, 52, 53, 55, 64
sales 13
scholars 5
scholarship 3
school 2, 3, 7, 8, 9, 10, 12, 15, 16, 17, 18, 19, 20, 21, 22, 23, 24, 25, 26, 28, 29, 31, 32, 33, 34, 36, 37, 38, 40, 42, 43, 44, 45, 46, 51, 52, 53, 54, 55, 56, 59, 60, 62, 63, 64, 65, 66, 67, 68, 69, 70, 71, 72, 73, 74, 75, 76, 77, 78, 80, 83, 84, 85, 87, 88, 89, 90, 93, 94, 95
schoolhouse 8
schools 3, 6, 10, 11, 19, 21, 26, 34, 54, 56, 57, 63, 69, 70, 71, 72, 80, 81, 86, 92, 94
scott 27, 28, 36, 37, 39, 40, 41, 42, 43, 44, 49, 52, 55, 57, 60, 61, 62, 63, 73, 76
secretary 1, 11, 46, 81
segregate 26, 63
segregated 2, 15, 16, 21, 69, 71, 75, 80, 84, 88, 89
segregation 2, 3, 6, 7, 8, 9, 11, 14, 16, 22, 23, 26, 28, 30, 33, 34, 38, 46, 47, 48, 53, 54, 56, 66, 67, 70, 71, 72, 77, 81, 83, 84, 86, 87, 88, 89, 94
segregationists 71
september 6, 12, 33, 34, 35, 52, 78, 80
sexism 88, 90
sexist 90, 92
sexual 92
shawnee 76, 77
shenanigans 72
sidney 61, 68
snell 58

south 2, 3, 7, 9, 14, 15, 16, 18, 20, 21, 22, 25, 28, 29, 31, 33, 34, 36, 43, 44, 49, 50, 59, 62, 63, 65, 66, 67, 68, 69, 70, 72, 73, 74, 75, 76, 77, 78, 80, 85, 88, 90, 91, 95

southern 26

southwest 6

spanish 7, 84

speer 5, 7, 8, 9, 10, 11, 13, 14, 16, 18, 19, 20, 21, 22, 23, 24, 81, 94

states 1, 6, 26, 86, 90, 91, 93, 94

statewide 67, 70, 71

storytelling 92

struggle 50, 53, 92

struggles 48

struggling 27

student 12, 13, 78

students 2, 3, 8, 13, 20, 21, 25, 31, 32, 34, 41, 43, 52, 53, 59, 60, 66, 68, 69, 70, 75, 76, 77, 78, 84, 85, 89

suffered 25

suffering 15, 61

suffrage 91

summers 7, 13, 84

sumner 77

supremacy 88

supreme 1, 10, 25, 36, 40, 52, 58, 60, 62, 63, 68, 69, 70, 71, 72, 75, 77, 78, 80, 85, 88, 89

swan 7, 16, 17, 19, 22, 23

swirk 6, 12, 84

sympathizers 9

systemic 89

T

tutor 59
tutors 66
two-room 8

U

umbrella 21
unacceptable 19
uncompromised 89
unequal 19, 26, 56, 84
unincorporated 7
united 1, 6, 34, 86, 90, 91, 93, 94
university 7, 84
unopposed 77
unprecedented 86
unpublicized 87
unsegregated 72
unsung 5, 82, 86
unwavering 59
utilities 52, 64

V

values 12
venetian 31
verdict 44, 65, 74
vernon 17
vicious 23
victimized 49
victory 3, 72, 78
violated 3
violation 56, 63
violent 21
virgil 17

voluntarily 71, 75, 76
volunteer 64
volunteered 18
vote 33, 51
voted 46, 48, 54
voters 23
voting 1, 92

W

walker 2, 8, 16, 17, 18, 22, 25, 28, 31, 32, 34, 43, 53, 59, 63, 65, 67, 69, 70, 71, 72, 73, 75, 76, 78, 84, 85, 88, 89
walls 31
war 7, 13
warning 22
warrant 43
watchmaker 6, 12
wave 91, 92
waves 91
webb 10, 17, 18, 22, 23, 25, 65, 80, 87, 89, 93
welder 10, 80
wetmore 54
wichita 36, 46, 47, 48, 54, 60, 66, 67, 68
wife 55
william 18, 19
williams 3, 27, 28, 29, 36, 37, 40, 41, 42, 43, 47, 48, 49, 50, 51, 52, 54, 55, 57, 60, 61, 62, 63, 65, 66, 68, 69, 70, 71
winter 5, 7, 8, 9, 10, 11, 20, 22, 24, 81, 94
wired 41
wisecup 17
witnessed 13
witnesses 87

woman 2, 6, 21, 49, 82, 83, 91
women 16, 37, 40, 42, 92, 93
wooden 8
workers 6, 7, 12, 13, 84
working 1, 10, 13, 44, 48, 80
wyandotte 18

Y

year 8, 14, 15, 55, 68, 73, 78
year-old 16
years 5, 6, 7, 10, 13, 19, 84, 93, 95
york 9, 27, 29, 58, 63, 92
yorker 58
young 6, 7, 12, 13, 55, 83
youngstown 68

Z

zone 24, 26
zoned 24
zones 24, 26
zoning 23, 63

The proceeds from the purchase of this book
support the mission of the
Faith and Public Policy Institute
to educate the faith community on
domestic and foreign policy.
Thank you.

www.ingramcontent.com/pod-product-compliance
Lightning Source LLC
Chambersburg PA
CBHW072005090426
42740CB00011B/2095